COUNTRY HOUSES

of

ENGLAND SCOTLAND AND WALES
A GUIDE AND GAZETTEER

ANDREW GINGER

GEORGE
PHILIP

For Alice

Published in 1991 by George Philip Limited
59 Grosvenor Street, London W1X 9DA

Text © Andrew Ginger 1991
Artwork © George Philip Limited 1991

British Library Cataloguing in Publication Data

Ginger, Andrew
    Country houses of England, Scotland and Wales.
    1. Great Britain. Country houses. Visitors' guides
    I. Title
    914.104859

ISBN 0-540-01221-1

Page design Janette Widdows
Typeset by BAS Printers Limited,
Over Wallop, Hampshire, Great Britain
Printed in Hong Kong

———◆———

Title-page illustration *An autumn view of Newby Hall in North Yorkshire*

Contents

The Morning Room at Waddesdon Manor, built to house Baron Ferdinand de Rothschild's 18th-century art treasures

Introduction

◆

The country houses of Britain are a unique heritage. Each forms a testament to a now-vanished way of life, and visiting them offers an opportunity to understand the social and cultural world of our ancestors.

The purpose of this book is to provide the would-be visitor with a concise, yet detailed, context from which to draw a picture of the social, architectural and artistic trends which shaped, changed and evolved the country house over six centuries.

The book is organized in the following way:

Origins A brief 16-part history, contrasting the various architectural styles with the changing daily habits of the aristocracy to show how the life style and self-perception of the noble classes were frequently reflected in planning, design and ornament. Sections on service, craftsmanship and the estate show how the local community staffed and crafted the buildings and maintained the grandeur their owners sought to project in all areas of life.

Gazetteer An alphabetical list of 100 selected country houses across England, Scotland and Wales, drawing, where possible, parallels to the architectural and social origins previously mentioned. Of the houses chosen, some are privately owned, while others are maintained for the public, but all have been chosen for their interest, originality or charm.

Maps Each of the houses described in the gazetteer is marked in red on one or more of the four preceding regional maps. In addition, six of the entries in the gazetteer have been specially selected to feature as a 'Guided Tour', receiving a more detailed study; these six houses are denoted on the maps by red capital letters.

Glossary A concise explanation of architectural terms.

Practical information is also given concerning opening times, and there is a comprehensive index.

◆

I
Origins

—◆—

When visiting a country house it is easy to assume that it is nothing more than a 'stately home' created purely for private enjoyment. The great mansions of Britain, however, were built not merely as dwellings, but as 'power houses' to display the status and wealth of the owner. From the fortified strongholds of the Middle Ages to the extravagant palaces of Victorian industrialists, the country house reflected social trends and the role of the aristocracy in society. Our ancestors were in no doubt as to what such houses stood for: to tenant farmers they expressed the inviolable strength of the ruling classes, and to noble neighbours they spoke of the subtle differences in rank and culture of their owners.

The history of the country house is a long one, stretching back to the manors mentioned in the Domesday Survey, compiled for William I some 20 years after the Norman Conquest of 1066. The word 'manor' comes from the old French *manoir* meaning dwelling, and it described the feudal community which farmed an estate in vassalage to a lord. Vassals held land belonging to the lord and received his protection in return for allegiance and homage; they were bound in service not just to farm, but also to fight for him if necessary. The lord's house gave security and protection to all the people living on the manor, and it was fortified to act as a stronghold to defend the community from attack.

Feudalism began to decline in the 14th century, and the strong government of Henry VII, who came to the throne in 1485, put an end to the business of private armies and large bands of retainers. From the end of the 15th century, therefore, lords were forced to adopt a more courtly role. Fortifications became cosmetic or disappeared altogether and new styles in domestic architecture developed. This new freedom coincided with the impact of the Italian Renaissance – an intellectual movement which challenged the religious conservatism of the Middle Ages. Renaissance writers promoted the idea of the scholarly courtier whose status was reflected in his intellectual command of the classics rather than martial skills. At first Renaissance influence in Britain was in diluted and often debased form, but the ensuing passion for the classical past lasted in various guises well into the 19th century.

Left *The west front of Knole, one of the largest houses in England*

From the Tudor period onwards, the country house became the centre for the national system of rural law and order; many members of the gentry sat as Justices of the Peace (JPs) in the shires and were selected for the post by the Lord Lieutenant of the county – usually one of the highest ranking peers of the county. So although the great landowning magnates no longer maintained vast private armies, each remained king in his own county. Entering into the political and legal system in this way was one of the ways in which the gentry effected an advance up the social scale, and increasing prestige was often accurately reflected in architecture. Much of the endless country house building, rebuilding, enlargement and refurbishment was part of a process of architectural one-upmanship. A change in fortune for a gentleman at court or the marriage of an heir to a grander heiress might be expressed by the addition of a portico, the construction of a new wing, or even by the building of a completely new house.

Royal preferment brought patronage and wealth, and many a great house was built or furnished out of the spoils of public service. Indeed, servants of the Crown expected rewards well beyond their salary. BURGHLEY HOUSE (Cambridgeshire), for example, was built by Lord Burghley out of a fortune amassed as Lord Treasurer to Elizabeth I, and KNOLE (Kent) was given by the Queen to her cousin Thomas Sackville (later Earl of Dorset) and subsequently furnished from royal cast-offs in the late 17th century.

By the Victorian period the Industrial Revolution had brought a rival form of wealth, independent of the possession of land. Wealthy businessmen invested in estates as a social convention, but had no sympathy with the old rituals associated with lord and tenant. Changes in agriculture resulted in more efficient farming with fewer rural workers, and the aristocracy began to lose its political grip on society. By the beginning of the 20th century, the country house was at its peak of luxury and sophistication in terms of planning, comfort and staffing, but social and economic changes have made the traditionally grand way of life increasingly difficult to sustain. Hundreds of country houses have been destroyed or converted to use as institutions of some kind, but it is remarkable how many are still in the hands of the families who built them. Visiting them represents a unique way of appreciating and reliving our past.

◆

BUILDING THE MEDIEVAL AND TUDOR HOUSE

Built for a community rather than a family, the typical medieval country house centred on a great hall, with outbuildings and the gatehouse clustered around an open courtyard. This type of plan remained unchanged in essence for over three centuries. The most important room was the hall, for this was the place

Bay windows in the courtyard of Little Moreton Hall – an excellent example of a half-timbered Tudor building

in which the lord's retainers ate, slept and lived. The earliest wooden halls have not survived, but from the 12th century walls were made of stone, and halls were sometimes aisled and decorated in a manner similar to churches.

Smoke from the central fire billowed up towards a louvred vent in the centre of the roof. Windows were small and shuttered, without glazing. To prevent draughts from the door blowing smoke about, two short wooden screens were placed beside each door and these in time grew into a continuous wooden structure with doors or curtains, creating the space known as the *screens passage*. Three doors opened from the screens passage and these led to the kitchen, pantry and buttery. The balcony above, known as the *minstrel gallery*, was used by musicians who played at feasts and festivals. At the opposite end of the hall to the screens passage was a dais set up from the rest of the hall, where the lord and his family would dine in state away from the messy floor. This section of the hall would be lit by a more sophisticated window – sometimes an *oriel* (a raised bay window) filled with stained glass. Adjacent to the dais, and often linked by a small private stair, was the great chamber, to which the lord would retire after the meal, and in which he slept.

The entrance to the hall was the principal focus of the house, and leading to it there was often a gate protected by a tower. In the days when private, feuding armies presented a great threat to a house, its fortifications were a vital part of its structure. Manor houses were equipped with battlements, drawbridges, moats and portcullises, although, as time went by, these features became more decorative than practical. Exterior walls were thick and robust, perforated only with arrow-slits and *machicolations* (projecting shutes along the battlements through which missiles could be dropped on to the heads of assailants). Houses of this sort are quite common; HEVER CASTLE (Kent) and COTEHELE HOUSE (Cornwall) give a good idea of their former defensive strength.

If buildings were not of stone, they were timber-framed. Such houses were constructed with a sophisticated timber skeleton infilled with a mixture of clay, twigs and hair known as *wattle and daub*. Although originally simple, the structure grew more complicated in the 15th and 16th centuries. The myriad of gables and bays of houses like LITTLE MORETON HALL (Cheshire) show how sophisticated such wooden building technology became. Wattle and daub was replaced in the 15th century first by *laths* (narrow strips of wood used to provide a framework for plaster), and then by Dutch bricks, particularly where local stone was not available to provide structural strength. The combination of brickwork and timber framing is called *nogging*, and it is the extra weight upon the timber beams that accounts for the picturesque sagging that we see today in houses of this type.

The Tudor dynasty (1485–1603) marks a watershed in English architecture in various ways. The Reformation virtually brought an end to church building, so domestic architecture became the main expression for the building boom that

The portcullises and drawbridge at Hever Castle in Kent

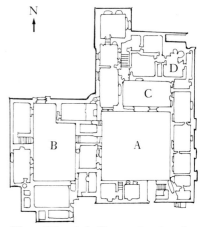

Plan of Cotehele House, showing the courtyard (A), retainers' court (B), hall (C) and kitchen (D)

peace and prosperity encouraged. At the same time, a transformation took place in style, as Renaissance ideas and decorative motifs were grafted on to medieval traditions.

It took a long time, however, for the idea to take root that the architect was a skilled artist rather than a master craftsman. Often we do not know who was responsible for the design of a house, and it is likely that some patrons, such as Sir John Thynne at LONGLEAT (Wiltshire), played an active part. Pattern books were used as sources for details, and classical motifs were often piled up with more enthusiasm than understanding, as in the bizarre entrance at LYME PARK (Cheshire). However, if the houses of the period sometimes lack finesse by purist standards, they certainly do not lack vitality, and buildings such as BURGHLEY HOUSE (Cambridgeshire) and MONTACUTE HOUSE (Somerset) are among the great glories of English architecture.

The outstanding architect of the period – indeed the only well-defined architectural personality – was Robert Smythson (*c.* 1535–1614), who is known to have worked at LONGLEAT, HARDWICK HALL (Derbyshire) and several lesser (but still highly impressive) houses. He broke away completely from the medieval tradition of designing a house around a courtyard, so his buildings are said to be 'outward-looking' rather than 'inward-looking'. His houses are massively compact rather than sprawling, often exploiting the dramatic effects of height and strong silhouettes. At LONGLEAT, the visitor still enters into the great hall through the screens passage, but the hall is now the impressive central room in a vast solid structure. More radical still was the plan of HARDWICK HALL, where the hall is turned through 90 degrees and runs through the complete width of the house. To the average Tudor yeoman, this must have seemed overwhelmingly modernistic.

LONGLEAT, HARDWICK HALL and other houses of the time are noteworthy for their extensive use of glass in large windows – they are often referred to as 'lantern houses'. Nothing displays better the nobility's understanding of the new power game than their almost reckless use of this still-expensive material.

◆

LIFE IN THE MEDIEVAL AND TUDOR HOUSE

The community which formed the typical medieval household – from about 1200 to 1500 – lived, worked and slept in one place. The heart of the house was a large, lofty hall with a central fire and rows of trestle tables, where such a gathering could be easily catered for. There was no effective artificial light, so the medieval day was based on the hours of daylight. Breakfast was between 6 and 7 am, and dinner – the main meal of the day – was between 11 am and noon.

OTHER MEDIEVAL AND TUDOR HOUSES

Further examples of medieval and Tudor houses planned around a central courtyard can be seen at Hengrave Hall (Suffolk) and Oxburgh Hall (Norfolk). The most spectacular example of the Tudor fashion for dominant gatehouses is Layer Marney Tower (Essex), while the Elizabethan 'E'-plan house around a central hall can be seen at Chavenage (Gloucestershire) and Castle Ashby (Northamptonshire). Robert Smythson's work is well represented by Burton Agnes Hall (Humberside).

Visiting such halls today – good examples are at PENSHURST PLACE (Kent) and STOKESAY CASTLE (Shropshire) – you have to imagine them full of choking smoke and festive din. The floor of the great hall was known as the 'marsh' because of its dirty appearance; the Dutch scholar Erasmus, who visited England in the first decade of the 16th century, vividly described how such floors were 'strewed with rushes, under which lie unmolested an ancient collection of beer, grease, fragments, bones, spittle, excrement of dogs and cats and everything that is nasty'. Above the 'marsh' sat the nobleman on the dais, under a canopy of state – as much to protect him from the effects of the birds in the rafters as to convey the majesty of his position – attended by his grooms and manservants.

Rank and hierarchy were reflected in the seating plan of the great hall. The tables nearest the dais went to the steward and the clerk of the kitchen, and the lower servants, or yeomen as they were known, occupied tables in descending order of importance. Eating was a matter of orderly chaos. In the absence of plates, food was eaten by hand from slices of stale bread put together to form a 'trencher'. After a great number of main dishes a 'banqueting course' was served. This came to be known as 'the dessert' because it was the custom for those at the high table to desert the hall at this point and take their assortment of sweet-meats and wines elsewhere. Later, banqueting houses would be built in the garden as at MONTACUTE HOUSE (Somerset), or on the roof as at LONGLEAT (Wiltshire) and HARDWICK HALL (Derbyshire).

By 1500, and the reign of Henry VII, Renaissance sensibilities were producing a change in manners. The breakdown of martial strength among the aristocracy meant that the nobleman no longer needed to identify with his retainers to the same extent. The noble family desired more privacy and sought to avoid the chaos, noise and evil smell of the hall, except for special feasts, transferring the centre of their activities to the great chamber on the first floor. This large room contained the state bed and here the lord slept and dined, and the rituals of homage were performed. Medieval nobles were treated almost like gods by their gentleman servants, who were drawn from the local lower aristocracy and gentry. The rituals of serving breakfast, for example, were specified in detail, with servants having designations such as 'gentleman cupbearer'. Each servant would kiss each item of cutlery and tableware before it was used. Dinner was served in the great chamber after high mass with the same reverence and ritual.

A further development of the 16th century was a growth in the sensitivity to etiquette and table manners. Books appeared on how to behave at meals, and diners were exhorted not to blow noses in tablecloths, spit on the rushes or into the cauldron over the central fire, or scratch violently if at all possible.

By the late 16th century, in the reign of Elizabeth I, the comforts of the great chamber were formalized by the removal of the state bed to its own bedchamber. The great chamber was now used as a proper formal dining room, for the lord,

STOKESAY CASTLE'S SOUTH TOWER

ORIEL WINDOW

Penshurst Place in Kent, particularly famous for its unaltered medieval hall

the upper servants and important guests. A withdrawing room was created as a private, comfortable living room for use after dinner, with other parlours created for informal day use. Thus the idea of a suite of formal apartments was created, and the hierarchy associated with the lord reinforced.

James I succeeded Elizabeth I in 1603 and immediately set about pruning and reorganizing the antiquated and cumbersome household he had inherited. This paring down of the household system and the further movement away from public displays of state spelled the end of the hall as the central room of the house. Hereafter the hall was little more than a reception room, a vestibule, and was frequently absorbed architecturally into the staircase hall.

PALISADE AT BLENHEIM PALACE

THE 17TH-CENTURY HOUSE 1610–1710

Inigo Jones (1573–1652) was one of the greatest of British architects and without any doubt the most influential. He was the first to have a complete understanding of classical architecture and the first architect to be regarded as an intellectual. His buildings are superbly lucid and harmonious, depending for effect on beauty of proportion and absolute rightness of every detail, rather than on sheer scale or abundance of ornament. His radical genius quickly established the idea of one individual credited with the planning and detail of every part of a structure as part of a coherent creative plan.

Jones seemingly began his career as a painter, although no paintings certainly by him are known, and from 1605 to 1640 he devoted much of his energies to designing the scenery and costumes for masques (dramatic entertainments with music and dancing) at the courts of James I and Charles I. His quarrels with his collaborator, the great dramatist Ben Jonson, showed how fiercely Jones was devoted to his art, refusing to yield precedence to Jonson's poetry. He did not emerge as a serious architect until he returned in 1614 from the second of two journeys to Italy. There he thoroughly absorbed the style and teachings of the great Italian architect Andrea Palladio (1508–80), and in 1616 he began the Queen's House in Greenwich, the first of his revolutionary buildings.

Unfortunately, a large amount of Jones' work as an architect has been destroyed or altered, and his only major work to survive at a country house is at WILTON HOUSE (Wiltshire), where his exact share in the design is uncertain. Although WILTON may not be purely by Jones, it is certainly worthy of him and illustrates an important point about his attitude towards architecture. He believed that although the exterior of a building ought to have a certain gravity ('solid, proportionable according to the rules, masculine and unaffected' is the way he expressed it), the interior could be much more festive, with the imagination 'licentiously

TRIUMPHAL ARCH AT WILTON

An overdoor painting of the great Inigo Jones, seen in the Blue Velvet Room at Chiswick House

flying out'. This is indeed the case at WILTON, where the south front is severe and almost unornamented, but the Single and Double Cube Rooms within are extremely luxurious and heavily decorated. This contrast between outward sobriety and inward show became a commonplace in British domestic architecture.

The new classical movement Jones had initiated was continued by his assistant and relative by marriage John Webb (1611–72) and by his friend the talented gentleman amateur Sir Roger Pratt (1620–85). At THE VYNE (Hampshire) Webb used the first temple portico to appear on an English country house – a feature which was later to be a standard expression of aristocratic magnificence. Pratt created the classic type of Restoration house, with steep roof and dormer windows – grand, but with a 'no nonsense', unpretentious air. Unfortunately, his few buildings have all been either destroyed or substantially altered. The main survivor is KINGSTON LACY (Dorset).

Pratt's buildings show some Dutch influence, and this became common in the late 17th century, notably in the smaller type of red-brick house often called after Queen Anne. With their simple pedimented façades and delightful contrast between red brick and white stone dressings and window frames, such Queen Anne houses are the quintessence of tranquil domesticity; ANTONY HOUSE and PENCARROW (both in Cornwall) are lovely examples. The name of England's most famous architect, Sir Christopher Wren, is often optimistically attached to houses of this period, but in fact no country house is securely documented as being his work.

Wren's two great younger contemporaries – Nicholas Hawksmoor and Sir John Vanbrugh – were, however, involved in country house design and were the chief figures in the fairly brief period when the Baroque style made a strong impact in Britain. This style is characterized by rhetoric and flamboyance. It originated in Rome in the early 17th century and is most associated with Catholic countries. CASTLE HOWARD (North Yorkshire) and BLENHEIM PALACE (Oxfordshire) are the great showpieces of Baroque architecture in Britain – huge, self-confident and uncompromisingly ostentatious. In Britain, the Baroque style appealed mainly to the rich, conservative Whig landowners, but it soon became increasingly apparent that the style went against the essentially conservative grain of the English aristocracy, and sobriety once again predominated.

OTHER 17TH-CENTURY HOUSES
Many country houses have work implausibly attributed to Inigo Jones, and there are only a very few instances where his participation in the design seems likely, notably in a pair of pavilions at Stoke Park (Northamptonshire). Winslow Hall (Buckinghamshire) is the likeliest country house attribution to Wren. Vanbrugh's dynamic Baroque style can be seen at Kimbolton Castle (Cambridgeshire), where he remodelled a Tudor manor house, and Seaton Delaval Hall (Tyne and Wear), a comparatively small house, but showing his style at its boldest.

———————◆———————

PALLADIANISM AND NEO-CLASSICISM 1715–90

The year 1715 was a highly important one in the history of taste in Britain. It saw the publication of the first instalments of two works that marked a turning point in architecture. These were the first English edition of Andrea

The first English country house to have a temple portico was The Vyne in Hampshire

*The ante-room at Syon House,
designed by Robert Adam, is a colourful
and extravagant piece of work*

Palladio's *Four Books of Architecture*, and a collection of engravings of contemporary British buildings entitled *Vitruvius Britannicus* ('the British Vitruvius', Vitruvius being a 1st-century BC Roman writer on architecture). The latter work was by the Scottish architect Colen Campbell. The two publications were key works in promoting Palladianism, a style of architecture based on the buildings and writings of the great Andrea Palladio, who had earlier been the decisive influence on Inigo Jones. Palladio's buildings are lucid, majestic, without any kind of excess, and based on a deep love of the architecture of ancient Rome. The Palladians tried hard to imitate his scholarly precision and dignity, but whereas the buildings of Palladio himself are warm and alive, those of his less talented admirers are often frigid and rule-bound. Apart from Colen Campbell, the leading Palladians included Giacomo Leoni (who published the translation of Palladio's treatise), Lord Burlington and William Kent.

The Percy lion atop Adam's gate at Syon House

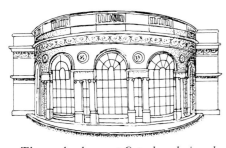

The garden house at Osterley, designed by Robert Adam in about 1780

In Britain, Palladianism was almost entirely a movement in domestic architecture. Palladian houses typically form compact blocks, with all the important rooms on the first floor (or *piano nobile*, as Palladio called it) above a *rusticated* base. (Rustication is the effect given to stone when it is rough-hewn or cut into deep channels, rather than finished smooth; such treatment helps to make the base of the house seem stronger and more robust.) There is often a central entrance portico with giant columns, approached by a twin-flight staircase, which takes the visitor above the level of 'the rustic'. Lord Burlington's CHISWICK HOUSE (London) is a good example of this arrangement. Wings consisting of additional smaller blocks were very often attached to the house by colonnades or curved corridors, and were intended to hold domestic services or further private suites. Symmetry and correctness of detail were overriding stylistic concerns. The fondness for book-learning and respect for authority was satirized by Alexander Pope, who (referring to Burlington) wrote: 'Yet shall (my Lord) your just, your noble rules, /Fill half the land with Imitating Fools'.

Just, however, as Inigo Jones (a hero to the Palladians) allowed himself much greater licence in interiors than exteriors, so Burlington, Kent and others were less rigid (although still eminently dignified) when designing the insides of their houses. Kent designed some of the most impressive interiors of his time, for example at HOLKHAM HALL (Norfolk), and he was the first to conceive of furniture as a part of a total ensemble with the architecture.

Kent also had an enormous impact in the realm of garden design in that he initiated the move away from formality in English gardens to a new idea of contrived nature – a classical landscape of grassy meadows to complement the classical house. In Kent's footsteps followed the great landscape gardener Lancelot 'Capability' Brown (1716–83), so-called because he would assess a landscape he had been asked to work on and say that it had 'capabilities'. He developed Kent's ideas of using clumps of trees and open lawns to make a natural effect.

The Sculpture Gallery, designed by Robert Adam, at Newby Hall

The spirit of Palladianism soon fired another generation to look for inspiration further back than Palladio to the remains of ancient Rome itself. Before the middle of the 18th century there had been little serious archaeological excavation, but the gentlemen dilettanti who enjoyed the Grand Tour discovered that the Romans were far more daring in both architecture and decoration than even Palladio had supposed. By studying and reconstructing the ruins as they were uncovered, the scale of Roman buildings and the complexity of their decoration was revealed.

The two dominant British architects of the late 18th century, Sir William Chambers (1723–96) and Robert Adam (1728–92), found much of their inspiration in these revelations. While Chambers was generally more sober in his approach, Adam worked out a new vocabulary of classical decoration of great beauty and refinement that made him the most popular architect and decorator of his time (he designed comparatively few country houses from scratch, but did a great amount of remodelling). The light ornament he introduced was based on the 'grotesque' painting of Pompeian murals. Swags of flowers, stylized honeysuckle and gently scrolling leaves, moulded exquisitely in plaster around painted panels, were components of this elegant style.

Adam went even further than Kent in conceiving an interior as an artistic unity. He was a brilliant ornamental designer and supervised the furnishing of his houses down to the last detail – even the door locks. His work was immensely influential and Sir John Soane, a leading architect of the next generation, wrote: 'the light and elegant compartments in the ceilings of Mr Adam, imitated from Ancient Works in the Baths and Villas of the Romans, were soon applied in designs for chairs, tables, carpets, and in every other species of furniture.' He worked in collaboration with leading painters, such as the Swiss-born Angelica Kauffmann, and with the finest craftsmen of the day, such as Thomas Chippendale. Probably no other architect or designer's work is encountered so frequently in British country houses as Adam's. His standards were so unfailingly high, his mind so constantly inventive that it is impossible to choose a 'greatest' or 'most representative' work, but CULZEAN CASTLE (Strathclyde), KEDLESTON HALL (Derbyshire), NEWBY HALL (North Yorkshire) and SYON HOUSE (London) are among the most famous.

OTHER 18TH-CENTURY HOUSES
The rival to Burlington's Chiswick House is Mereworth Castle (Kent) by Colen Campbell, which was likewise designed in imitation of Palladio's Villa Rotunda. A typical Palladian house – a rectangular mass with four corner towers – can be seen at Lydiard Park (Wiltshire). Robert Adam's work is found in a great number of houses; the larger ones are famous, but there are also comparatively little-known delights such as Ugbrooke House (Devon), which is intimate in scale.

LIFE IN THE CLASSICAL COUNTRY HOUSE

After the hall ceased to be the principal eating room, the country house altered in plan. In the mid 17th century the great chamber – now the formal dining room – was moved downstairs, placed beyond the entrance hall and renamed the saloon. It was used for eating, dancing, and festivities such as feasts or banquets. From this time to the mid 18th century most houses were planned in this way – the hall and saloon aligned at the centre of the house with a staircase off to one side. CASTLE HOWARD (North Yorkshire), KEDLESTON HALL (Derbyshire) and HOLKHAM HALL (Norfolk) are all examples of such a layout.

The great Baroque houses of the late 17th century and early 18th century were built to impress by a sense of scale and drama. The stately suites of apartments, which had first appeared in the late 16th century, were laid out in the manner of the French palace at Versailles – that is to say, in a long line, one room opening on to another, the doors all aligning to form a vista. The grandest houses had two such *enfilades*, as this kind of axial sequence is known, radiating from the saloon at the centre of the house. These state rooms were frequently built with the King and Queen and their retinue in mind, in the hope that Their Majesties would some day grace the noble family with a visit. Lesser families entertained important guests in their more modest state bedrooms. The arrangement of the rooms reflected the formality and etiquette of the court, and beyond all the endless ante-rooms and withdrawing chambers always lay the state bedchamber, accessible to only a privileged few. Beyond this lay the closet – a small sitting room or study that was the only place where a noble could escape to complete privacy. The formal rooms were built to impress, and state beds were always the most lavish and valuable piece of furniture in the house. In his state bed, draped with heavy curtains to shut out the draughts and endless procession of passing servants, the visiting grandee rested in sublime comfort, while the noble host was accommodated in similar, though far less lavish rooms elsewhere in the house.

By their very nature such state rooms were little used, and, once the era of regal entertaining had passed, they quickly became superfluous and used purely for show or antiquarian interest. As the 6th Duke of Devonshire mused in 1844, how much more comfortable CHATSWORTH (Derbyshire) might have been if the state rooms, which occupied the best rooms of the house with the best views of the park, had been converted to use by the family rather than left merely for pointless display.

The family's everyday rooms were usually in the rusticated ground floor or basement of the house. The novelty of the Palladian house was that the state rooms above were used for entertaining a company of people rather than one grand guest, and also for displaying the art treasures amassed by the family. From the middle of the 18th century the dining room, or eating room as it was then known, emerged as a separate room used purely for eating, while the other rooms – music room, library, drawing room – were placed around the saloon in such a way that guests at a function could do a circuit. HOUGHTON HALL (Norfolk), HAREWOOD HOUSE (West Yorkshire) and KEDLESTON HALL are examples of such a plan.

The library in the country house had begun as the private domain of the scholarly gentleman in the late 16th century, but during the 18th century the informality and cosiness of the room led to its use as an all-purpose day living

An early example of a state bed, as used by James I at Montacute House

The chimneypiece in the Marble Hall at Kedleston Hall

The magnificent library at Kenwood is claimed to be one of Adam's greatest works

room. The emphasis from the 1770s on greater privacy and comfort brought the creation of many similar 'common' rooms for domestic functions – morning rooms, studies and boudoirs reflect the urge to enjoy a relaxed intimacy before entering into the long and complex business of dressing, making-up and powdering for the late-morning walk or visit. The drawing room was used primarily in the evening after dinner, but was also the place where morning callers would be treated to the pleasurable ritual of tea. Tea drinking, which began in the late 17th century, was an expensive and exclusive custom, a pound of tea in the 1720s costing about one hundred times as much as it would at today's values. No wonder, therefore, that tea caddies were lockable, or that servants made a clever racket out of peddling recycled tea leaves. The hour of dining grew later and later in the 18th century, partly because of better lighting techniques, but mostly because of the increase in convivial evening sociability in late 18th-century London. The main meal had been served at 2 pm early in the century in both town and country, but the hour of dining grew progressively later in London, until by the 1770s it was about 4 or 5 pm. The men joined the ladies for tea and coffee in the drawing room after the drinking of port and madeira wines, and indulged in the civilized pastimes of cards and conversation until supper was brought in at 10 or 11 pm.

In the Victorian period, gaslight and the developed sense of social ritual placed dinner squarely in the evening, with the custom of supper rendered unnecessary. Dining rooms in the 18th century had been painted in light colours, and frequently lacked chandeliers because they were primarily used at the time of maximum daylight. The Victorian dining room was prone to rich, dark colourings and the room made the most of the decorative potential of candle- and gaslight from sconces, candelabra and chandeliers. The Victorian house was planned for comfort and informality, with formality reserved only for dinner and large functions. Luncheon was introduced early in the 19th century to fill the gap between breakfast and the similarly new afternoon tea.

———◆———

LATE GEORGIAN
AND REGENCY HOUSES 1790–1830

The future George IV was Prince Regent from 1811 to 1820, but as applied to the arts the term Regency is used more broadly and vaguely, covering the period from about the beginning of the century up to his death in 1830. The Prince Regent led fashion in architecture as he did in other areas of taste, most notably in the showy, outlandish exoticism of the Royal Pavilion at Brighton. In this period the classical tradition of the late 18th century diversified into a number of sub-styles, including the Indian and Egyptian, and classical taste was

Right *Sir Walter Scott's palatial house at Abbotsford, built in the 'Baronial' style*

itself developing into the severe, restrained Greek Revival, the outcome of further archaeological discoveries.

Another strand of taste in this complex network is represented by the 'Picturesque' movement, which flourished at the end of the 18th century and the beginning of the 19th century. Devotees of the Picturesque took delight in roughness and irregularity, so the type of buildings favoured were asymmetrical and preferably rugged in texture. Medieval castles, of course, fitted this description and there grew a vogue not only for garden follies masquerading as ruined towers, but also for whole buildings in a rather manicured castellated style. This Regency Tudor Gothic, which can be seen at such houses as BELVOIR CASTLE (Leicestershire), was quite different from the more scholarly Victorian Gothic Revival (into which the style gradually developed) and bore only a generalized relation to known medieval forms. The point of it all was visual effect. Usually there was no attempt to carry the medieval theme through to the interiors of such houses, where the decoration was uniformly classical. In Scotland, Sir Walter Scott created an individual type of pseudo-medieval house for himself at ABBOTSFORD (Borders). The 'Baronial' style, as it became known, proved extremely popular north of the border.

India, Britain's most important overseas possession, was a place where careers and fortunes could be made, and a land with an extremely rich cultural tradition, so it is not surprising that it should influence taste in the mother country during a period that represented something of a stylistic free-for-all. Interior decoration was becoming progressively more exotic with the use of beautiful Indian fabrics and chintzes, imported in vast numbers from the 1780s onwards. A few years later, in 1803, Sir Charles Cockerell, a rich businessman who had recently returned from India, chose to build an Indian 'pleasure dome' in the Cotswolds. SEZINCOTE (Gloucestershire) was the result – a masterpiece of Picturesque effect – and it was this house which inspired the Regent to transform his then classical Pavilion at Brighton into an oriental fantasy. The Regent's pleasure dome was not completed until the 1820s, by which time bamboo designs and other aspects of Indian and Chinese exoticism had been incorporated into domestic ornament.

Apart from these two outstanding works, however, there were no other major buildings in the Indian style, and the classical tradition continued to be at the core of British architecture. Archaeological discoveries had led to a yet greater awareness of Greek and Roman interiors and furnishings, and knowledge of these was spread through various publications. One of the most influential was *Household Furniture and Interior Decoration* (1807) by Thomas Hope, a collector, patron and writer who came from a wealthy banking family and could therefore indulge his interests to the full. He designed Greek- and Egyptian-style furniture himself and trained craftsmen to make it for him. The taste for things Egyptian had begun in the mid 18th century, but did not become widespread until

INDIAN PAVILION AT SEZINCOTE

EGYPTIAN-STYLE TABLE

**OTHER EARLY
19TH-CENTURY HOUSES**
The Regency Tudor Gothic style – the precursor of the more scholarly Victorian Gothic Revival – can be seen at its most extravagant at Dalmeny House (Lothian), while the exotic strain in Regency architecture is well represented in the Mogul conservatory at Alton Towers (Staffordshire).

stimulated by Napoleon's Egyptian campaign in 1798. Apart from Thomas Hope, Thomas Chippendale the Younger was among those interested in Egyptian taste; he made furniture in the style for STOURHEAD (Wiltshire).

———◆———

VICTORIAN AND
EDWARDIAN HOUSES 1837–1914

The Victorian age was one of huge technological advance and vast population growth, of rampant self-confidence and vigorous expansion. Engineering achievements conquered the difficulties of travel and revolutionized the processes of building. Many new country houses were built for wealthy entrepreneurs keen to acquire the respectability that came with land and property.

Victorian architecture is noteworthy for its remarkable stylistic variety, and this is probably more apparent in houses than in any other type of building. For a patron who was wealthy enough it was more or less possible to have any style that took his or her fancy applied to the structure of the building. Gothic, Hindu, Flemish, Moorish, Venetian and Elizabethan were all on the menu in this stylistic banquet. Sometimes there were associated reasons for the choice of a particular style, such as at WADDESDON MANOR (Buckinghamshire), which was built in a lavish French Renaissance style for Baron Ferdinand de Rothschild, a great collector of French art.

The only true constants in the homes of the very wealthy were their size and their amazing domestic complexity. The progressive ideas of comfort and informality led to the creation of new rooms – smoking rooms, billiard rooms, conservatories and boudoirs – all of which allowed the guests at the now-popular house parties (a new institution resulting from the railways) to indulge specific interests and enjoy leisure to the full.

Servants increased in number, and the distinctions between master and servant grew more rigid than ever before. Houses were planned in such a way that no member of the family or guest should inadvertently happen upon a member of staff. 'It was the affectation of the time,' wrote one writer early in the 20th century, 'that work was done by magic.'

Although there was so much stylistic revivalism in the period, Victorian architects showed that new life could be injected into old traditions. Even the Gothic style, which had had so many variations played on it over the centuries, proved capable of fresh interpretations, most notably in the hands of William Burges (1827–81). Greatly inspired by the Pre-Raphaelite painters, Burges created the kind of building in which their dreams of medieval romance could be played out, with an abundance of heavily-carved ornamentation. It was, naturally, extremely

ONE OF THE THREE FATES AT
CASTELL COCH

Waddesdon Manor, built in 1874–89 in the French Renaissance style

OTHER VICTORIAN AND EDWARDIAN HOUSES

The Victorian passion for the vast and the imposing is vividly illustrated at Carlton Towers (Humberside), which has a clock tower that rivals Big Ben. Knightshayes (Devon) shows William Burges in a more domestic mood than Castell Coch, although the house has been used as the set for a film of *The Hound of the Baskervilles*. Standen (West Sussex) is one of the many fine examples of houses by Philip Webb, who along with Richard Norman Shaw led the way from period revivalism to a more informal domestic style. The interior decoration includes much work by William Morris. The twilight of the great country house building tradition is represented by Sir Edwin Lutyens, whose work includes Castle Drogo (Devon), the last great medieval-style house (1910–30).

WHITE MARBLE BATH AT
CHATSWORTH

expensive, and only Lord Bute, said to be the richest man of his time, had the money and the inclination to put such fantasies – at CASTELL COCH (South Glamorgan) – into solid form on a large scale.

The most brilliant architect of country houses at the end of the Victorian period was Richard Norman Shaw (1831–1912), who had just about every quality an architect could desire. He was a superb draughtsman, a good organizer, a born diplomat with clients, and a master of even the most prosaic details of his profession (he was knowledgeable about drains, for example). He was also highly imaginative and showed that it was possible to create completely individual buildings by combining various features and traditions from the past. A fine example is CRAGSIDE (Northumberland), combining timber framing with stone and taking full advantage of the spectacular site.

When they were not creating vast houses from scratch, the Victorians were endlessly rebuilding, extending and altering, and few country houses escaped some sort of Victorian adjustment. Some houses, such as CHARLECOTE PARK (Warwickshire), were completely aggrandized in a romping Tudor style, while others, such as HEVER CASTLE (Kent), were saved from ruin by boldness of vision and sensitivity of craftsmanship.

World War I, which ended the line of many families and changed forever the rural economy, also sealed the fate of the country house way of life, and after 1920 very few large examples were begun. Squeezed by increasing maintenance costs and a limited social role, the country house by the 1940s came to symbolize a past way of life.

◆

BELOW STAIRS: SERVANTS AND THE COUNTRY HOUSE

Good pay, relatively easy work, the provision of food, clothing and security, and the chance of advancement made service in the Middle Ages a much sought-after profession. Some of the rank and prestige of the noble was extended to his household, and the livery of a great family was worn with pride by their most humble retainers. Such loyalties were very much part of the old feudal system, whereby the lord protected the household (which often amounted to a private army) as though it were an extension of his family. After the shift away from military strength among the nobility, the landed classes maintained their superiority through legal and financial might.

A major household before about 1600 was divided into a host of miniature hierarchies, each dominated by a gentleman officer of the household. The steward ran the household, the gentleman usher maintained the state apartments and

*The servants' hall at Erddig, complete
with portraits*

18TH-CENTURY PLATE-WARMER

OTHER DOMESTIC AREAS
Berkeley Castle (Gloucestershire) has
an impressive medieval kitchen and
the one at Cawdor Castle (Highland)
was in use as early as 1640. An 18th-
century kitchen can be seen at Sulgrave
Manor (Northamptonshire), and
Manderston (Borders) has a complete
basement showing the intimate below-
stairs working of a great Edwardian
house. Castle Drogo (Devon) has one of
the first kitchens to be designed down
to the last detail by a major
architect (Lutyens).

received visitors, the gentleman of the horse ran the stables, and so on. These
were posts of great prestige and little manual work. Such posts developed a web
of interest among the yeomen servants who constituted the lower ranks, and who
served the lord and worked the estate. These humbler servants slept in the rushes
on the floor of the great hall or on truckle beds which folded away in the corridors
of the house.

To distinguish one household from another, servants wore a livery. Gentlemen
wore cloaks and yeomen coats which had the crest or coat of arms of the noble
employer clearly emblazoned upon them. This 'labelling' emphasized the sense
of belonging experienced by the medieval servant. By the 17th century, livery
had all but vanished (except for footmen) and the servant was turning into a paid
employee. The footman was to become the most fundamental part of the staff
in the 18th century, and also a vital part of carriage equipage. Originally footmen
were employed to run behind the carriage as a kind of mobile bodyguard. They
became very fit and were often raced competitively for wagers. They graduated
over the years to the tasks of welcoming guests and waiting at table.

The 18th-century household bore no comparison with its medieval predecessor.
The servants ate in the servants' hall in the basement and slept in the garrets
in dormitories. Those at ERDDIG (Clwyd) are a remarkable survival of the sort
of accommodation staff could expect. The gentlemen servants had vanished and
had been replaced by the butler and the housekeeper. The distance in rank
between the noble and his servant grew ever wider, while at the same time the
emergent middle classes were creating an enormous number of new domestic jobs.

An average staff in the Regency period consisted of 20 to 40 servants, and the
domestic routine was very refined. Maids rose at 6 am in winter, an hour earlier
in summer, and were soon busy laying fires, dusting and sprinkling wet sand
on carpets ready for sweeping, before the family rose. Coal had to be brought
to all the fires, all the floors were polished with beeswax, and water had to be
transported for baths. It was all intended to run like clockwork, according to the
housekeeping manuals of the day, even to the extent that housekeepers knew the
exact hour when the sun shone directly into the grand rooms, threatening to
damage the fine fabrics and paintings. A maid would be dispatched to lower the
blinds at the appropriate time for each room in the house.

In the Victorian period, service became yet more efficient. The vast mansions
of the Victorians were staffed by large numbers of hard-working servants, who
toiled in underground passages and service corridors. The household in this period
was organized so that female servants avoided contact with the male – to be found
in any kind of compromising situation brought instant dismissal. The outdoor
staff consisted of stable personnel to maintain the carriages and horses, parkmen,
woodsmen, keepers and gardeners. The complexity of staff areas in these houses
often led to the creation of a service wing of equal size to the house.

After World War II such servant wings were largely uninhabited. Service declined as a fashionable employment and the unsociable hours and demanding life style were abandoned by many in search of better things. Houses such as ERDDIG, SALTRAM (Devon) and CALKE ABBEY (Derbyshire), with their preserved kitchens and staff quarters, summon up something of the life and experience of the people who kept the country houses in smooth running order.

◆

FURNITURE 1400–1700

The medieval house was simply and sparsely furnished. The commonest piece of furniture was the coffer, a storage chest usually made of nothing more than six cut timbers with a hinged lid. Such chests held virtually everything, from clothes and linen to valuable personal effects. In addition to the coffer, grander rooms had an aumbry or hutch – this was a little cupboard often pierced with Gothic motifs such as *quatrefoils* (roundels with four lobes). Chairs were very rare before 1600, and usually reserved for the lord of a house or very important guests. Other members of the household sat on long benches, which accompanied the trestle tables of the great hall, or else on sturdily-made stools. In the great chamber, prior to the 16th century, the lord ate from a makeshift 'board' covered with a cloth. From the late 16th century small tables were made for this purpose and some of the best examples of such tables are at HARDWICK HALL (Derbyshire), extremely heavy and densely carved with mythological beasts. Beds were symbols of state and grandeur and were always hung with heavy cloth, partly to keep out the draughts endemic in any house of the period, and partly to guarantee privacy from passing servants.

In the 16th century a new piece of storage furniture was created. The court cupboard, used to store and display the lord's valuable plate, consisted of a carved oak cupboard with a carved canopy supported by two small turned columns. The backboard was usually heavily carved with figures, heads or geometrical patterns. In 1620 the first dining chairs appeared. They had upright backs and took their form from the common stool of the period. Chairs of a cross-frame pattern, with a high back and a large tasselled cushion, became common as thrones or chairs of state; some examples of this early type remain among the furniture collection at KNOLE (Kent).

The increase of literacy towards the end of the 17th century produced a number of new forms of furniture intended for use when writing. A simple form of portable writing slope had existed since the late 15th century, but it was now ornamented with legs and fine veneers to make a decorative piece of furniture. The scriptor, which appeared in the 1670s, was a large chest containing little drawers and

LINENFOLD PANEL AT THE VYNE

Left *The staircase at Knole shows Jacobean craftsmanship at its very best*

pigeonholes, with a large ornamented fall-front and long turned legs. In the 1680s the chest of drawers, which had first appeared in simple form in the 1650s, was married to the desk to form the bureau, and from this base the familiar bureau-bookcase and secretaire developed.

While the earliest pieces had been decorated with carving of biblical scenes or allegorical subjects, in the early 16th century new patterns developed. 'Linen-fold' was a representation of draped cloth, and it appeared on wall panelling and coffers. Inlay, an art perfected by the Romans, was rediscovered at about the same time. Bedheads and chests were frequently treated with black and white designs of bog-oak and holly, either in geometrical patterns or in an architectural fantasy of towers and turrets – said to have been inspired by Henry VIII's palace at Nonsuch, demolished in the 17th century. The Jacobean period saw a movement in carving and decoration away from the heaviness of the Elizabethan period to simple patterns of gouging, arcading and *strapwork* (carved ornament resembling curling straps of leather).

The Commonwealth (1649–60) was a period of austerity in England, and ornament of any kind brought disapproval from the ruling Puritans. The Restoration of Charles II in 1660, however, resulted in a sudden flamboyance – the cane-backed chairs of the 1680s are a riot of scrolls and flowers, with cherubs supporting ostentatious carved crowns. 'Barley-sugar-twist' legs and shaped stretchers were also common.

Dutch marquetry – more pictorial and complex than previous English examples – exerted a great influence in this period, and after the arrival of Huguenot (French Protestant) exiles in the 1680s and 1690s much fine marquetry furniture was produced. The Glorious Revolution of 1688, which brought the deposition of James II and the accession of William III and his wife Mary (James's sister) from Holland, increased the Dutch influence at this time, notably in glamorous veneering in richly patterned woods such as walnut. Perhaps the most significant import of all from Holland was the 'S'-scroll support which appeared everywhere and in the remaining years of the century evolved slowly into the *cabriole* leg. This type of leg – curved outwards at the 'knee', tapering inwards below and terminated with a foot shaped like a claw or similar feature – was one of the most distinctive features of 18th-century furniture design.

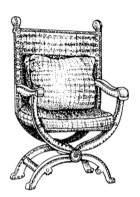

EARLY 17TH-CENTURY STATE CHAIR

OTHER MEDIEVAL FURNITURE
Fine walnut and oak furniture of the 16th and 17th centuries can be seen at Otley Hall and Kentwell Hall (both in Suffolk) and Michelham Priory (East Sussex). Poundisford Park (Somerset) has excellent Elizabethan furniture, and pieces showing the best of 17th-century craftsmanship are at Stanford Hall (Leicestershire) and Breamore House (Hampshire). An appropriately furnished Jacobean hall is at Trerice (Cornwall), and exceptional late 17th-century pieces can be seen at Tredegar House (Gwent).

FURNITURE 1700–1900

The Queen Anne period (1702–14) brought new restraint in the decoration and form of English furniture. The 'bell-backed' chair, with cabriole legs, was the height of fashion. This form of chair is noteworthy for the way in which

The exquisite chinoiserie 'tea party' in the Chinese Room at Claydon House

*A fine Adam-style mirror above the
fireplace in the boudoir at
Belton House*

every part is subtly curved to contribute to the design. The back curves as it rises from the seat in the usual 'spoon-back' fashion to cup the upper part of the sitter's body; it also curves laterally to give yet more comfort and support. Carcass furniture was usually veneered in walnut and enhanced by crossbanding with other woods in geometrical patterns.

The harsh winter of 1709 had a profound effect on the course of English furniture. A vast number of walnut trees died, so that by the 1720s seasoned stocks were running very low, and cabinet-makers were forced to turn to an alternative wood which would be able to take veneer work and also adapt to crisp carving. Mahogany, first shipped in from the West Indies as ballast, was ideal and it was imported in bulk after 1725. The new wood arrived at the same time as the Palladian school of architecture (see page 18) was at its height and mahogany was perfect for the architectural details which decorated the heavy furniture associated with Palladianism. Moreover, the dense, straight grain of mahogany made it possible to carve a more slender, more graceful cabriole than ever before.

The rococo movement, which arrived in England in the 1740s and 1750s, fostered a sprawling, asymmetrical fantasy style of interlaced 'S' and 'C' scrolls, leaves, flowers and rockwork. Much of the design was influenced by *chinoiserie* – the passion for all things oriental which had first appeared at the end of the 17th century. It was common to find mirrors, wall-sconces, tables, beds and chairs carved with little pagodas, fretwork and Chinamen amid the omnipresent rococo foliage.

Perhaps the most famous designer of this style was Thomas Chippendale (1718–79). In 1754 he produced *The Gentleman & Cabinet-Maker's Director*, a pattern book with instructions for the making of his sophisticated designs. At a stroke, Chippendale reached a large new market of patrons and an even larger audience of craftsmen. He had such an enormous influence that the term 'Chippendale' is applied to furniture in his style, as well as to pieces produced in his own shop. He did not stamp or sign his furniture, but bills and receipts have sometimes been preserved, and several houses – including HAREWOOD HOUSE (West Yorkshire), NOSTELL PRIORY (West Yorkshire) and NEWBY HALL (North Yorkshire) – have Chippendale furniture authenticated in this way.

Chippendale published two further editions of his book, in 1755 and 1762, in which the designs grew progressively more neo-classical. His neo-classical work was as pure and refined as his rococo work was flamboyant; motifs such as fluting, medallions and sphinxes beautifully complemented the Adam rooms for which his pieces were specifically designed.

George Hepplewhite (died 1786), a neo-classical designer who contributed a great deal to the early Regency style, followed Chippendale's lead by bringing out a pattern book, posthumously published in 1788 (with revised editions in 1789 and 1794). It was entitled *The Cabinet-Maker and Upholsterer's Guide*.

Stained-glass design by William Burges for Castell Coch

Hepplewhite's style was light, delicate and more curvaceous than the earlier Adam style. He introduced the shield-back chair into the English drawing room as well as popularizing elegant painted furniture. No furniture can be attributed to Hepplewhite himself.

Thomas Sheraton (1751–1806) is the third of the trio of famous names that dominated 18th-century English furniture. He, too, brought out an influential pattern book, *The Cabinet-Maker and Upholsterer's Drawing Book*, published in parts between 1791 and 1794, and two other similar works. Frequently made in lightweight satinwood, with its rich yellow colouring, Sheraton furniture was made portable in keeping with Regency ideas on practicality, so that ladies could arrange furniture to suit themselves. Like Hepplewhite, Sheraton is not known to have made furniture himself (he published religious tracts as well as furniture designs and became a Baptist minister in 1800, going insane four years later).

Excavations in Greece and Egypt at the very end of the 18th century produced a new type of neo-classical furniture, characterized by very solid architectural forms. Thomas Hope (see page 28) led the way, and his designs were scaled down for the average home by George Smith. Sphinxes, griffins, and hairy-paw feet were common features, and darker woods, such as rosewood, with its black and reddish veins, were used in conjunction with ormolu gilding. Although very little furniture was actually made by Thomas Hope, there is hardly a piece of Regency furniture which does not, in some small way, reveal the influence of his ideas.

At the end of the reign of George IV, machine technology had begun to encroach upon the traditional methods of furniture production. Mass production for the prosperous middle classes, mechanical carving techniques and more advanced veneer saws brought prices down and tended to lead to heavy, over-decorated furniture. The decadence of taste which had begun in the Regency period continued in the Victorian, with a passion for exotic richness and sumptuous show. Perhaps the best of Gothic Revival furniture, which took many forms, was that produced by William Burges for houses such as CASTELL COCH (South Glamorgan), where dressing tables are cast as miniature fortresses and painted maidens look out of every pigeonhole.

The most important and influential craftsman-designer of the Victorian period was William Morris (1834–96), who in 1861 founded a firm producing furniture, tapestry, carpets, stained glass, wallpaper and so on. He tried to revive the idea of the medieval guild, in which the craftsman designed as well as made the work, and he set himself against machine production. Like Burges, he was influenced by the Pre-Raphaelites and loved romantic medieval themes. His entirely hand-made products are of superb quality and it is an indication of the lasting popularity of his designs that his wallpapers are still commercially produced today.

OTHER 18TH- AND 19TH-CENTURY FURNITURE

One of the finest collections of English furniture in Britain, of all ages but particularly rich in 18th-century pieces, is at Temple Newsam House (West Yorkshire). A good range of items of all ages can be seen at Burton Agnes Hall (Humberside), and particularly good late 18th-century craftsmanship can be seen at Powderham Castle (Devon) in the rooms built by James Wyatt in the 1790s. The collection of Gillow furniture at Leighton Hall (Lancashire) – home of the Gillow family – provides an exceptional range of the best of Regency styles. Leith Hall (Grampian) has a large collection of 18th- and 19th-century furniture.

*The bed in the Queen of Scots
Dressing Room at Chatsworth*

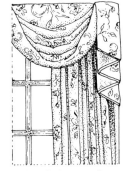

*'Swag and tail' drapes, first seen in
the 1790s*

FABRICS IN THE COUNTRY HOUSE

The earliest focus for material lavishness and luxury in the country house was the state bed. In the earliest houses, the state bed was at the climax of the suite of rooms positioned and decorated to display the status of its owner, and therefore warranted the spending of huge sums on its decoration and furnishings. The famous bed made for CHATSWORTH (Derbyshire) in 1697, now to be seen in the long gallery at HARDWICK HALL (Derbyshire), represents the height of the 17th-century upholsterer's art. Scrolling, upholstered woodwork, grand drapes and elaborate detailing make it a superbly ostentatious piece. Similarly, the Spangled Bed at KNOLE (Kent), made for James II, shows the finest materials extravagantly used. It was in the design of such beds and their testers that swags, bells, tassels, box pleats and choux decorations first appeared, later to become the decorative vocabulary of curtain design in the 18th century. The use of cut velvet and silk appliqués for a simple outline gave way in time to the Palladian style, which favoured a grand architectural frame. The state bed at HOUGHTON HALL (Norfolk), designed by William Kent, is just such a bed, with a bold architectural cornice, huge shell motif and rich hangings in green velvet edged with silver lace.

By the 1740s, bed design was moving into the domain of the cabinet-maker and the upholstery was less important, except on very special pieces such as the famous OSTERLEY PARK (London) bed by Robert Adam – a neo-classical *tour de force* complete with dome and sumptuous fringing. In the 1760s the Polonaise bed became fashionable, featuring a dainty dome supported on four curved posts hung with extremely theatrical drapes and a riot of swagging, bows, frills and fringing. Examples of such beds can be seen at CHATSWORTH and DRUMLANRIG CASTLE (Dumfries and Galloway).

Before the late 17th century the idea of window curtains was little known. They first appeared in the 1670s and 1680s in bedrooms and dressing rooms. By 1700 there were three distinct types: the ordinary draw curtain, the reefed curtain and the festoon curtain. Reefed curtains are drawn up at the sides to form two swags like a stage curtain, whereas a festoon curtain is drawn up vertically by strings to form a number of little swags. Grander rooms in the mid 18th century nearly always had festoons. They were made to hang in such a way that when they were drawn up they hung clear of the architrave of the window, allowing its architecture to be completely uncluttered. Festoon curtains came to be the height of fashion and were made in heavyweight materials such as velvet, and lightweight taffetas, depending on the desired effect.

By the 1790s festoon curtains had been replaced with rod curtains. These allowed the use of a dramatically draped pelmet, and the popular 'swag and tail' arrangement appeared at this time. The drapery was made to look as though it had been casually looped over an ornate pole a number of times and then left to hang in folds at each end. In reality each piece of drapery was made separately

The ornate Spangled Bedroom at Knole in Kent

OTHER ORIGINAL FABRICS
State beds with original hangings are on show at Beningborough Hall (North Yorkshire) and at Clandon Park (Surrey), where wall damasks have also survived. A late 17th-century bed and bedroom suite in original damask upholstery can be seen at Powis Castle (Powys). William Morris fabrics can be seen at Standen (West Sussex).

Stone vase in the grounds at Wimpole Hall

and carefully cut, folded and attached with lavish use of tassels, fringing and gilded pole enrichments to complete the effect. A particularly splendid example is at SEZINCOTE (Gloucestershire). During the Regency period ever more spectacular and heavy drapery became fashionable and began to lend itself to vulgar ostentation. The arrival of chintzes (printed glazed cottons) from India encouraged the trend towards colourful displays of drapery, particularly in bedrooms. Tented rooms, in which the walls and ceiling were covered with fabric, were common in this period. This rich use of fabric continued well into the Victorian period, and it was not until the Edwardian period that the fashion for more simple drapes influenced interior decoration.

GARDEN BUILDINGS

Most country houses in Britain have some kind of garden building, be it a folly, ruin, gazebo, eyecatcher or temple. They were often whimsical, exotic or bizarre in style, for, unlike the country house itself, the garden buildings were inspired by a delightfully romantic idea of the past – temples and monuments were a way of bringing the dream of ancient Rome to the modern landscape, while some features reflected the nostalgic intoxication of the Middle Ages. Others still were exotic, a pseudo-Chinese style being particularly popular – part of the general taste for chinoiserie. Another strain is represented by the idea of the 'rural idyll', *cottages ornées* (rather artfully rustic buildings) being designed to reflect this dream.

The first garden buildings were the banqueting houses used in the 16th century for taking dessert on summer evenings. Many are simply rooms on the roof, like those at HARDWICK HALL (Derbyshire) and LONGLEAT (Wiltshire). Others, however, are genuine ornamental garden structures, such as the pavilions at MONTACUTE HOUSE (Somerset). 'Hunting stands' were often erected in parks in this period to watch the spectacle of the chase, and the 'Hunting Tower' at CHATSWORTH (Derbyshire) was possibly the first of such permanent structures, which in time became belvederes and hunting lodges.

The development of the concept of the landscape garden was part of the Picturesque movement, which demanded that landscape be judged and planned by the same criteria as landscape paintings, and in accordance with its ideals garden buildings took on a new importance. The idyllic paintings of Claude Lorraine (1600–82) were particularly revered, and the types of buildings they showed – temples, ruins, bridges – were taken as models. William Kent was the originator of the circuit garden walk interspersed with temples, statues and cascades; the most famous example of this is the garden at STOURHEAD (Wiltshire).

The Pantheon sits beside the lake at Stourhead, amid beautiful gardens

OTHER GARDENS WITH BUILDINGS

The most extensive landscape gardens are at Stowe (Buckinghamshire), which boast the astonishing figure of 32 major garden buildings ranging from classical temples to a Chinese tea house. A pretty shell cottage and a Temple to Diana can be seen at Adlington Hall (Cheshire), while temples and gazebos are at Blair Castle (Tayside), Dalemain (Cumbria) and Burton Agnes Hall (Humberside).

The Gothic style was inspired by the romance of ancient castles and monastic ruins. It was quite unscholarly, but had a lightness and charm all its own. The ruin at WIMPOLE HALL (Cambridgeshire) is an excellent example of a folly in this style. In 1743, one writer described such ornamental buildings as 'the habitations of fairies . . . the retreats for shepherds and owls'.

The rustic follies of the early 19th century sought to capture the simplicity of rural life and the charm of vernacular architecture. Queen Marie-Antoinette's *Hameau* (hamlet) in the grounds of the palace of Versailles was the epitome of this purely romantic style and here she daintily milked cows and tended carefully laundered sheep as an enactment of her rural dream. The 70-year-old Sir Harry Fetherstonhaugh of Uppark in West Sussex took the rural idyll so seriously that when he married an 18-year-old dairy maid in 1825, he built her an ornamental milking parlour as a gift.

PAINTINGS AND COLLECTIONS

The link between aristocratic status and the collecting of art began in England in the late 16th century. The new interest of that period in classical learning, intellectual achievement and art in all its forms changed the aristocrat from a feudal warlord to a glittering, gracious courtier, whose patronage of the arts revealed his refinement and nobility.

Before the 16th century, painting in country houses was of a purely decorative kind, and was similar to the murals and architectural decorations found in medieval churches. The parlour at LITTLE MORETON HALL (Cheshire) has a rare survivor of this kind of decoration, consisting of large areas of plaster painted to simulate ornately carved panelling, surmounted by a pictorial frieze showing a biblical scene. The frieze in the High Great Chamber at HARDWICK HALL (Derbyshire) is unusual for its high-relief plaster mouldings, but in its simple colouring (now quite faded) and naïve representations still identifies with the medieval tradition.

The dramatic change in the role of paintings in the country house came with the passion for collecting portraits in the 16th century. Houses developed galleries at about the same time as areas for exercise and leisure activities, and from the middle of the century portraits began to be hung in these long empty rooms as the most convenient place to enjoy and discuss art. Portraits in the Elizabethan period were something of a craze, and nobles were keen to acquire pictures of their friends, relations and monarch to express their political sympathies or connections. It was common to display a collection of portraits of kings and queens of England, or Roman emperors, to encourage contemplation while exercising.

Examples of such historical portraits can be seen in the gallery at MONTACUTE HOUSE (Somerset). Galleries became larger and more magnificent as they grew more fashionable and that at HARDWICK HALL, linked as it is to a very grand suite, was one of the most magnificent of its day and still holds many of its original portraits.

In the late 17th century the influence of the Baroque style produced a new role for decorative painting in the country house. Baroque architecture created dramatic effects of scale and illusion, well suited to the display of vast murals of gods and goddesses winging through cloudy skies. The aristocracy built vast palaces in imitation of the splendour of the French court and engaged a handful of *emigré* Continental muralists to add the dramatic paintwork. The Italian Antonio Verrio (*c.* 1639–1707) and the Frenchman Louis Laguerre (1663–1721) were the most in demand in the last quarter of the 17th century and were patronized extensively by the Crown at Hampton Court Palace and Windsor Castle. At BLENHEIM PALACE (Oxfordshire), Laguerre painted the saloon to depict a classical temple to which thousands appear to have thronged to gaze over the balustrade and witness the spectacle of the ducal dinner. Similarly Verrio's 'Heaven Room' at BURGHLEY HOUSE (Cambridgeshire) attempts to amaze with its dramatic crowd of gods and goddesses and stage-set scenery techniques. Sir James Thornhill (1675–1734) was the only English artist to practise with distinction in this field, and his work at BLENHEIM PALACE and CHATSWORTH (Derbyshire) brought him considerable fame.

Large-scale decorative painting was a fairly short-lived vogue in Britain, and by the time of Thornhill's death in 1734, the Baroque style had been virtually eclipsed by Palladianism. Decorative painting in architectural schemes continued, but in a less flamboyant and lavish way, in keeping with the cool, restrained classicism of the movement. William Kent (1685–1748), famous as an architect, landscape gardener and furniture designer, also had ambitions as a painter, although he was much less talented in this field: Horace Walpole said he was 'below mediocrity'. Examples of his work can be seen at HOUGHTON HALL (Norfolk) and ROUSHAM PARK (Oxfordshire), the latter using arabesque designs inspired by Raphael's Loggia in the Vatican.

After the 18th century there was not much mural painting in country houses, but there are some interesting Victorian examples at WALLINGTON (Northumberland) and an engaging modern attempt to revive the spirit of the past at RAGLEY HALL (Warwickshire). Just at the time when heroic decorative painting died out, however, the taste for collecting paintings (and other works of art) began to accelerate rapidly, and many of the country house collections most admired today have their origins in the 18th century. The true noble was now considered to be the connoisseur. Encouraged to go on lengthy Grand Tours to witness the finest art at first hand, the nobility returned with an array of paintings, sculpture

OTHER PAINTINGS AND COLLECTIONS

Examples of Baroque decorative paintings by foreign artists can be seen at Kimbolton Castle (Cambridgeshire) and Moor Park Mansion (Hertfordshire). Almost all country houses have some kind of picture collection, but some of them are of such high quality that they rank as important art galleries in themselves.

Among them is Alnwick Castle (Northumberland), which includes works by such illustrious artists as Titian and Tintoretto and one of the most breathtaking Van Dycks in the country (*Algernon, 10th Earl of Northumberland*). The most unusual feature of Buscot Park (Oxfordshire) is a room in which the wall panelling incorporates a lovely series of paintings on the story of Sleeping Beauty by the Pre-Raphaelite painter Sir Edward Burne-Jones. Among the other artists represented at Buscot Park are Rembrandt and Murillo.

The view northwards along the long gallery at Hardwick Hall

and antiquities with which to ornament their new classical mansions. Many houses, such as CORSHAM COURT (Wiltshire), ATTINGHAM PARK (Shropshire) and NEWBY HALL (North Yorkshire), had special art and sculpture galleries added at this time, and in certain extreme cases, such as ICKWORTH (Suffolk), the house was secondary to the gallery.

Paintings were collected not only as cultural artefacts, but also as straightforward souvenirs. Many artists in Italy made their living almost entirely by catering to the tourist trade. Canaletto's clientele was mainly English and his views of Venice are in many country houses, notably WOBURN ABBEY (Bedfordshire). In a similar vein, his contemporary Giovanni Paolo Pannini specialized in views of Rome, particularly ruinscapes. Pompeo Batoni was the leading Italian portraitist of this period, and it was virtually obligatory for distinguished foreign visitors to Rome to have their picture painted by him, often shown against a backdrop of the Colosseum or some other ancient building.

COUNTRY HOUSE VISITING

The homes of the great families of Britain have always excited interest by their history, their architecture and their art, and the practice of visiting them has a long tradition. Aristocratic families have always opened their doors to tourists, usually as a symbol of genteel hospitality, but it was only in this century that the financial benefits of opening to the public have saved many houses from extinction.

Before the Reformation, visitors tended to be the pilgrims who travelled the country to worship at the principal shrines. Although pilgrimage was regarded as a religious duty, travel was very difficult and dangerous and the slow progress was usually broken by a short stay at a monastery or noble house, where the giving of hospitality was a matter of honour and position.

The Dissolution of the Monasteries from 1536 to 1539 provided large estates and accompanying fortunes for many of the aristocratic class. This resulted in a building boom which coincided with the arrival of Renaissance thought in England and its associated passion for architectural experimentation. Elizabeth I's courtiers vied with each other to build bigger and more beautiful palaces, and the visiting of houses by the aristocracy or gentry to praise or criticize became an accepted pastime. Celia Fiennes (1662–1741) travelled widely at the end of the 17th century as a genuine tourist, and she compiled a diary of her experiences. One of her principal enjoyments was the assessment of the great houses, where she was either greeted by a member of the resident family or shown around by a housekeeper.

Right The steps leading up to Kedleston Hall

In the 18th century, travel for its own sake became much more fashionable and the cult of the Grand Tour encouraged an interest in architecture and the appreciation of the art collections of the nobility. The growing middle class, who had access to both education and urban genteel society, were eager to identify with the governing élite, and so regarded the visiting of country houses as a most important way of exhibiting and developing their taste.

This sudden growth of visitors clearly put under strain the relaxed tradition of opening houses as a matter of hospitality. WILTON HOUSE (Wiltshire) received 2324 people in 1776, and Horace Walpole at the ever popular Strawberry Hill in Middlesex exclaimed: 'I am tormented all day and every day by people that come to see my house.' The sheer volume of people led to new problems for owners, such as thefts and damage – at BLENHEIM PALACE (Oxfordshire) the Dresden china had to be locked away after breakages were reported. In 1760, visiting at CHATSWORTH (Derbyshire) was limited to only two days a week, a restriction soon imitated by WOBURN ABBEY (Bedfordshire) and KEDLESTON HALL (Derbyshire). Tickets began to be issued, with rules of conduct attached; at Strawberry Hill, for example, 'those that would have tickets are desired not to bring children'.

Proper guidebooks were produced to satisfy the visitors' requests for accurate information. The guidebook at Stowe in Buckinghamshire was among the first in 1744, and that at WILTON HOUSE went through 26 editions between 1751 and 1798. Only a few of the great houses went quite this far, and most still relied on the abilities of the housekeeper as tour guide. Visitors would present their card at the gate of a grand house, and the housekeeper would schedule the times of tours, receiving a tip at the end. As visitors increased, some housekeepers earned a good income from this service, and in 1783 Walpole said that his housekeeper Margaret obtained such sums 'that I have a mind to marry her, and so repay myself that way'. Mrs Garnett at KEDLESTON HALL, one of the most visited houses in the 18th century, seems to have been the most professional tour guide of her age, and was lauded by visitors for her knowledge and civility.

It was in the 19th century that, despite fears of drunkenness and vandalism, social reformers succeeded in opening certain public buildings to the general public. These included Hampton Court Palace and in one year 115,971 visitors passed through its halls. *Bill Banks's Day Out*, published in 1868, satirized the reactions of many of these new tourists: 'We went through the different rooms, a-looking at the pictures and painted ceilings, and all that, and very nice they was, though we couldn't quite understand some of them, 'specially the ceilings, which were all gods and goddesses.'

Major houses all over the country began to open to the general public on specific days, and the growth of seaside tourism, formalized vacations and railway travel encouraged this. The National Trust was founded in 1894 by a group of architectural enthusiasts and nature conservationists who found that nothing was being done to protect the great historic houses of Britain and their treasures from deterioration and destruction. The saving of many outstanding houses by the Trust revolutionized attitudes to conservation and so encouraged private owners to form a commercial equivalent in the Historic Houses Association. These two bodies aim to ensure the survival of Britain's unique heritage and the contribution it makes to our understanding of history.

THE ESTATE AND THE COUNTRY HOUSE

The country house stood at the centre of an estate; it was the estate which created the wealth that made the house possible, and the estate which maintained it. Ownership of land was concentrated in the hands of a very few, and most estates were jealously guarded and passed down within the great noble dynasties. Acquiring an estate was therefore very difficult, as was realized by the 2nd Earl of Nottingham, who spent £50,000 buying an estate in 1681 and a further £30,000 erecting a house from scratch.

The estate was largely self-sufficient; in an age of poor transport, they had to be self-supporting. Before the 18th century, boat and ox cart were the chief means by which goods such as coal, wine and salt were transported. It was, therefore, essential that the butler regulate consumption of such items very carefully, as they could not be obtained at short notice. Sugar loaves, spices, tea, cloth and paper, if not bought in large amounts in London, were purchased at local fairs or from retailers in the nearest city.

DOVECOTE INTERIOR *c.*1685

Servants drank ale from earliest times, and this was usually brewed on the estate. Examples of brewhouses are rare today, but originally every house had one – a surviving example can be seen at CHARLECOTE PARK (Warwickshire). Meat was driven on the hoof to the house from its pasture on the estate, or, if a noble had land in different places, would be driven from one county to another. Country houses frequently had their own slaughterhouses, which, with the large amounts of meat consumed, were kept permanently busy – in 1671 the Duke of Bedford and his household of 40 at WOBURN ABBEY (Bedfordshire) consumed an average of seven bullocks a month.

In addition to cattle, the estate stocked a number of deer, which grazed in the park and provided a good deal of sport. The hunting lodges, often built at high points on the estate, provided a clear view of the chase over a large area of the park. The high brick or stone walls which surround most country houses today are the 18th-century replacements of the earlier wooden palings intended to confine the deer. Dovecotes supplied pigeons, and from the estate fishponds

SUFFOLK WAGON *c.*1880

An apple tree in the walled garden at Stonor Park

came a wide range of fish. The home farm was always near the house, although usually located out of sight, supplying milk, butter, cheese, vegetables, flour and potatoes. It was a convenient place for the 18th-century gentleman to experiment with new techniques to enlarge yield, and was a place of innovation. The most famous of these dedicated agricultural innovators was the celebrated 'Coke of Norfolk' at HOLKHAM HALL (Norfolk). An interesting re-creation of the breadth and diversity of the home farm can be seen at WIMPOLE HALL (Cambridgeshire).

The country house kitchen garden was the direct descendant of the monastic herb garden which grew herbs for medicine, cooking, dyeing and fragrance. Plants such as lavender were strewn around the floor in medieval times, a forerunner of today's pot-pourri. By the late 17th century, under the control of the head gardener, the kitchen garden produced vegetables, hard and soft fruit, and often more exotic crops such as peaches, oranges and lemons.

In the days before refrigeration, the difficulties of food storage resulted in a range of preserves, jams, pickles, salted meats, and smoke-cured joints and fish being produced throughout the summer months. Potted meat was invented at the end of the 18th century, and canned food arrived in the 1830s. Ice-houses were usually built in the grounds of houses and consisted of underground pits about 30 ft (9 m) deep, with stone or brick walls. Ice cut from the frozen lake in winter and kept in straw would last for up to three years in this way and was used to cool wine, make ice cream and keep meat fresh.

The biggest change to the organization of the country house and its estate came in the early 19th century when improved roads suddenly made all goods more accessible. Retailers could stock all the luxury goods the house needed on a regular basis, as well as the usual staples, removing the need for the house to maintain a slaughterhouse, and reducing the importance of the home farm, turning it progressively towards a commercial function. As with so many other facets of country house life, just at the point when supplying and maintaining the house grew most sophisticated and refined, the advances which had wrought these changes began the decline of that way of life itself.

OTHER ESTATE BUILDINGS AND KITCHEN GARDENS

Ice-houses can be seen at Killerton (Devon), Gosford House (Lothian) and Sutton Park (North Yorkshire). Walled kitchen gardens and herb gardens survive at Knebworth House (Hertfordshire), Parnham (Dorset) and Sudeley Castle (Gloucestershire). Cranbourne Manor Gardens (Dorset) feature several different types of gardens, originally laid out in the 17th century.

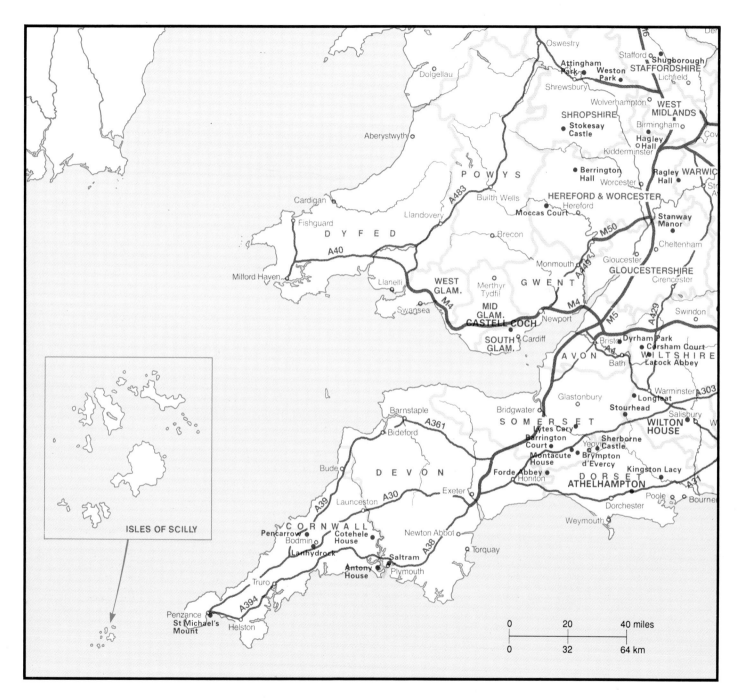

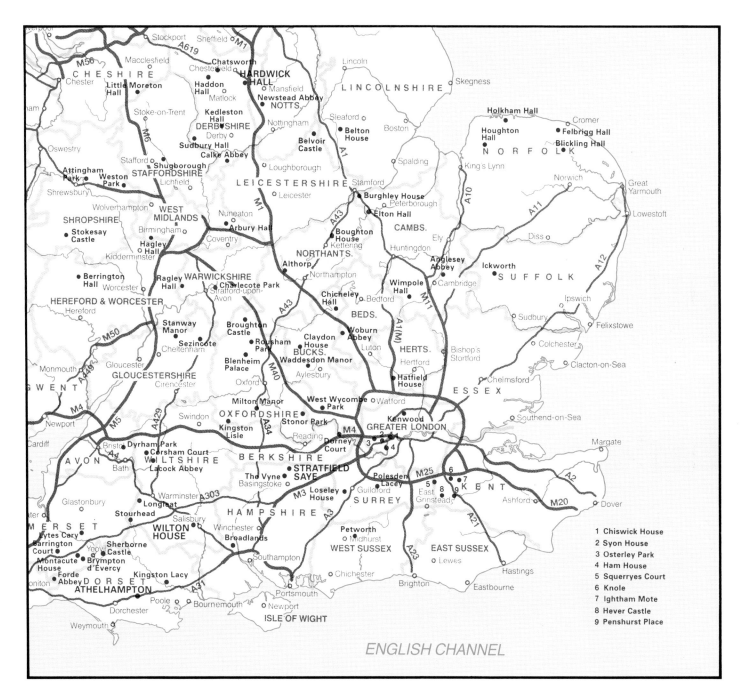

1 Chiswick House
2 Syon House
3 Osterley Park
4 Ham House
5 Squerryes Court
6 Knole
7 Ightham Mote
8 Hever Castle
9 Penshurst Place

ENGLISH CHANNEL

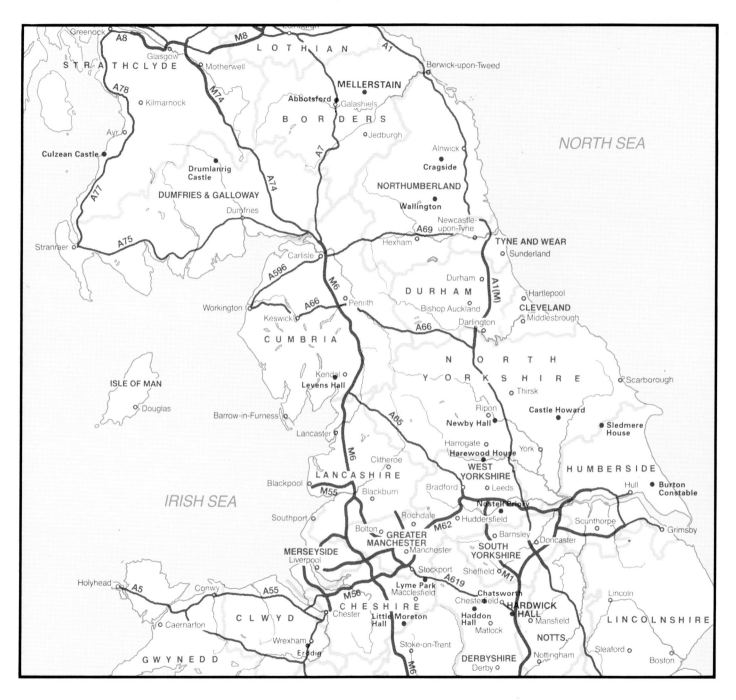

SCOTLAND

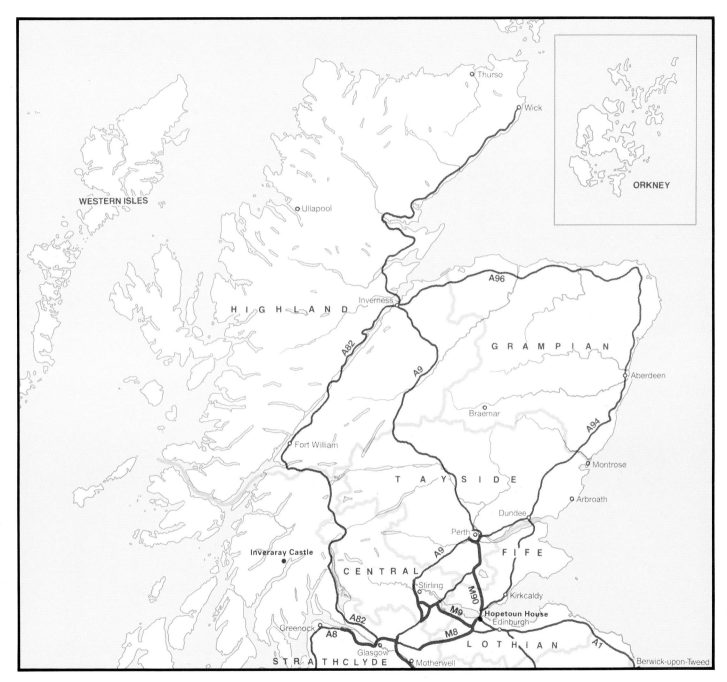

WESTERN ISLES

ORKNEY

Thurso
Wick

Ullapool

HIGHLAND

Inverness

A96

A82

A9

GRAMPIAN

Aberdeen

Braemar

A94

Fort William

TAYSIDE

Montrose

Arbroath

Dundee

Inveraray Castle

A9

Perth

FIFE

CENTRAL

Stirling

Kirkcaldy

M90

M9

Hopetoun House
Edinburgh

Greenock

A82

M8

LOTHIAN

A1

A8

Glasgow

STRATHCLYDE

Motherwell

Berwick-upon-Tweed

2
Gazetteer

ABBOTSFORD BORDERS

Sir Walter Scott (1771–1832) was a lawyer by profession, but he became enormously successful as a poet and even more so as a novelist. Most of his books dealt with Scotland's romantic history, and the large income they earned enabled him to live in the style of a medieval lord. In 1811 he bought a small farmhouse near Melrose: it was then called Clarty Hole, but he immediately renamed it Abbotsford. This he gradually developed into a palatial country house, complete with turrets, towers and battlements, which stood at the centre of a large estate. Scott went bankrupt in 1826 because of the collapse of a publishing house in which he had invested. He lived at Abbotsford for the rest of his life, however, and the house still belongs to his direct descendants. It was the most influential building in creating the 'Baronial' style that became the rage for country houses in Scotland in the 19th century. The designs were discussed with a number of artistic and architectural friends, but the look of the place was very much Scott's own creation.

Scott was an enormously popular man and the most famous Scotsman of his time. It was his writings, more than any other factor, that created the popular glamorous image of Scotland's history and landscape and in the process made the country a tourist attraction. He was an avid collector of historical relics and many of these can be seen at Abbotsford. In particular, the armoury contains a fine collection of arms and armour, including Rob Roy's sword and gun, given to Scott after his novel about the hero was

published in 1817. In the library, which contains over 9000 volumes, the ceiling ornaments are copied from Melrose Abbey and Roslin Chapel; they are in plaster, but grained to resemble cedar. There is a fine pair of 17th-century Venetian chairs here, carved in boxwood with florid Baroque detailing. The bust in this room was placed on its pedestal by Scott's son on the day of his father's funeral.

The study, where Scott wrote, contains yet more books, and connects secretly to his bedroom. The desk was made by Gillow in 1810. The armchair was presented to Scott in 1822, and was made from the rafters of the house of Robroyston, where in 1305 the Scottish patriot Sir William Wallace was arrested. Other fascinating relics include a lock of Bonnie Prince Charlie's hair, a pocket book belonging to Flora MacDonald (the heroine who helped the prince to

Abbotsford, the home of Sir Walter Scott

Left Antony House – a fine Queen Anne building

Althorp has been the home of the Spencer family since the early 16th century

escape after his defeat at the Battle of Culloden in 1746), and a clasp that fell, dramatically, from Napoleon's cloak in his carriage after his flight from Waterloo.

3 miles (5 km) west of Melrose, south of
the A72 (map page 56)

ALTHORP NORTHAMPTONSHIRE

Althorp (pronounced 'Althrup') has belonged to the Spencer family since 1508. Almost nothing can be seen of the Tudor parts of the house, however, for it was much enlarged and rebuilt in the 17th and 18th centuries, notably by Robert Spencer, 2nd Earl of Sunderland. He served Charles II and James II and then went on to hold high rank under William III. This remarkable tenure of royal service allowed him to amass a considerable fortune, and the foundations of the family art collection were laid at this time. The 3rd Earl married Lady Anne Churchill, daughter of the Duke of Marlborough, and a grandson from this marriage, who was created 1st Earl Spencer in the mid 18th century, engaged Henry Holland to remodel the house further in 1786.

Architecturally Althorp is dignified, but not one of the great houses of the country. When it comes to the collection of paintings, however, it has few rivals. Justly famous are the court beauties painted by Lely in the 1680s and Van Dyck's double portrait of the 2nd Earl of Bristol and the 1st Duke of Bedford. There is a whole room given to portraits of the family by Gainsborough and Reynolds – the tender portrayal of the Countess Spencer with her daughter Georgiana shows Reynolds at his very best. Georgiana was later to become a celebrity as the beautiful Duchess of Devonshire. There are many other works by leading 18th-century portraitists, as well as good examples of the 17th-century Dutch, Flemish and Italian schools.

The furniture collection at Althorp is also of high quality, boasting fine examples of Chippendale, Sheraton and William Vile, and a particularly splendid Louis XVI period cabinet by Adam Weisweiler, a German furniture-maker who settled in Paris. As proof that the Spencers have never done anything by halves, the dining room contains an astonishing 54 matching mahogany chairs!

Althorp has become particularly famous since the marriage of Lady Diana Spencer to the Prince of Wales in 1981 and the house was completely redecorated in 1982.

5 miles (8 km) north-west of
Northampton, west of the A428
(map page 55)

ANGLESEY ABBEY CAMBRIDGESHIRE

Anglesey Abbey was built in the 12th century as an Augustinian priory. After the Reformation the house passed through a number of families until it was rescued from ruin in 1926 by the highly cultured collector Huttleston Broughton, 1st Lord Fairhaven. He transformed the old house to form an interesting setting for his varied and extensive art collection, which includes furniture, paintings, sculpture and ceramics from many periods and countries. The result is a house with a remarkably eclectic interior, full of surprises and mixing ancient artefacts with 20th-century comforts.

There are many Gobelin, Mortlake and Soho tapestries at Anglesey, and paintings are hung throughout the house.

Anglesey Abbey houses an extensive art collection

The library is dominated by Constable's *The Opening of Waterloo Bridge*, and there are two outstanding Claudes. The other painters represented here include Bonington, Gainsborough and Etty.

The furniture is of a similarly high standard, and the roll-top bureau by David Roentgen (the greatest of 18th-century German furniture-makers) is particularly notable. The collection is arranged without regard to date or origin, but simply in those combinations desired by Lord Fairhaven. In this it resembles some of the grand houses of America's East Coast (Lord Fairhaven's mother was a New York heiress), lending the house a most distinctive and individual quality.

Near the village of Lode, 6 miles
(9.5 km) north-east of Cambridge, off
the B1102 (map page 55)

ANTONY HOUSE   CORNWALL

Built between 1710 and 1721 on the site of a Tudor house for Sir William Carew, Antony House sums up all that is most elegant about Queen Anne architecture. The fore-court is sheltered by two flanking pavilions topped with *cupolas* (little domes) and linked by arcades to the smooth, silver-grey mansion. Everything about Antony is simple, well proportioned and refined.

There is a certain romance about the Carews and the Pole-Carews who were always so deeply enmeshed in Cornish political affairs. Sir Alexander Carew, whose portrait hangs in the library, was one of the many people of his time who was tormented with uncertainty by the Civil War. He originally took the Parliamentarian side in the conflict, to the shock of his staunchly Royalist family. They tore the portrait from its frame – only to restore it with somewhat crude stitches, which are still visible today, after Sir Alexander's Royalist sympathies re-emerged. He was promptly executed by the Roundheads for this change of heart. A further moving reminder of this turbulent period is the portrait of Charles I in the entrance hall, painted at his trial by Edward Bower. One of several versions of the painting (another is at PENCARROW, Cornwall), it shows the King enduring the strain of his captivity, during which his beard turned suddenly grey.

A certain calm settled on Antony after these difficult times had passed, and in the 18th century the estate passed to Reginald Pole of Shute in Devon, and thence by descent to the present Sir John Carew Pole, who gave the house to the National Trust in 1961.

The panelled rooms contain many fine paintings, including portraits by Reynolds, Ramsay, Kneller, Lely and Michael Dahl (a Swede who settled in England in 1689). There is some fine Queen Anne furniture and in the tapestry room is a walnut table of the 1720s carved with unusual Red Indian heads. The Mortlake tapestries in this room are of a similar date. The oak staircase, a masterful piece of 18th-century woodwork, is lit by large, original, fishbowl candle lanterns.

2 miles (3 km) north-west of
Torpoint, north of the A374
(map page 54)

ARBURY HALL   WARWICKSHIRE

Arbury was one of the first houses to have an interior in the *Gothick* (fanciful 18th-century Gothic Revival) style. The complex and highly sophisticated plasterwork that adorns walls, ceilings, doorframes and windows is so whimsical, delicate and abundant that it brings to mind a giant wedding cake.

Sir Roger Newdigate (5th Baronet) inherited Arbury at the age of 14 in 1734, and began the redecoration of the house in 1750 – only a year after Horace Walpole had begun his innovative Gothick designs at Strawberry Hill. He left untouched the Elizabethan exterior of the house, but inside he sought the advice of architects Sanderson Miller, Henry Keene, and later Henry Couchman of Warwick, to create the effects he desired. Each of the principal rooms was re-decorated in sequence, and the work continued until Sir

Roger's death at the age of 87 in 1807. The detailing was inspired by the Perpendicular Gothic style, the fan vaulting, for example, being derived largely from Henry VII's chapel at Westminster Abbey. Many chimneypieces were modelled on Gothic tombs and in some rooms, such as the dining room, where sculptures stand under grandiose tracery canopies, there is an almost monastic atmosphere.

There are excellent paintings throughout the house, including a fine portrait of Sir Roger, sitting proudly in his handsome new library, by Arthur Devis. There are portraits by Hoare, Hudson, Lawrence and Romney, and a touching religious scene by Reynolds entitled *John the Baptist when a Boy*. Fine 18th-century furniture and beautiful Chelsea china contribute to the interest of the house.

2 miles (3 km) south-west of Nuneaton,
off the B4102 (map page 55)

ATTINGHAM PARK   SHROPSHIRE

The lofty, stately entrance front of Attingham looks out over a perfect landscaped park towards the village of Atcham. The house was designed in 1782 by George Steuart for the 1st Lord Berwick and incorporates parts of an earlier Queen Anne building, Tern Hall. Further additions were made by John Nash in 1805, when a picture gallery was created and a dramatic staircase formed at the heart of the house.

The entrance hall, which Steuart intended to open on to the staircase, but which Nash made into a separate unit, combines the work of both architects. The ornate neo-classical ceiling and *scagliola* work (plasterwork imitating marble) are by Steuart, but the *grisaille* (in shades of grey) paintings were Nash's idea. The room stands centrally between two ranges of apartments; the left-hand range incorporates the dining room and Lord Berwick's apartments, and the right-hand range has the drawing room and Lady Berwick's rooms, which terminate with a boudoir.

The drawing room is a sumptuous example of Regency taste with blue silk curtains and a suite of white and gold furniture that may have been made for Napoleon's sister, Caroline Murat. The boudoir is one of the finest rooms of its date in Britain; painted with scrolling decorative motifs by a French artist, Louis-André Delabrière, it is similar to work at Southill in Bedfordshire and the demolished London palace of the Prince Regent, Carlton House.

Nash's picture gallery was the first specially-designed top-lit gallery found in a country house, and its use of cast-iron ribs was technically avant-garde. Unfortunately, though not untypically for the innovative but impractical Nash, it was always prone to leaking. The ceiling now has an additional modern glazed roof.

The dining room, painted in red picked out with gold, has an exceptional plaster ceiling, complemented by the carpet of *c.* 1800. The chairs, which are original to the room, are fine examples of Regency design.

4 miles (6.5 km) south-east of
Shrewsbury, off the A5 (map pages 54–5)

BARRINGTON COURT   SOMERSET

In the long, flat valley that dominates this part of Somerset are located some of the most beautiful 16th-century houses in the West Country. Among them is Barrington Court, a mid 16th-century manor house built by William Clifton, a wealthy Norfolk merchant. The house is 'E'-shaped in plan and has rows of symmetrical mullioned windows and a skyline of twisted chimneys and finials.

Barrington Court dates from the mid 16th century

Continued on page 66

Guided Tour

◆

ATHELHAMPTON DORSET
This ancient seat, the legendary site of the palace of the Saxon king Athelstan, has been a home for over 1000 years. It belonged to a number of old Dorset families before it was acquired in 1485 – the year of Henry VII's victory at Bosworth Field – by Sir William Martyn, who immediately set about building a new manor house. Sir William was a man of considerable importance; he held a lucrative right to collect duty payable on wine, and was elected Lord Mayor of London in 1493.

The optimism of those early Tudor years is reflected in the main front of Athelhampton. It was originally built with a protective gatehouse (which was demolished in the 19th century), but Athelhampton's defences were little more than cosmetic.

The wing to the left of the great hall was added in the first half of the 16th century by Sir William's son Christopher. In 1595, four Martyn sisters inherited equal shares of the house. The eldest married

The entrance front of Athelhampton, a house built substantially at the start of the Tudor era, viewed from the south

Henry Brune, and the house remained in Brune possession until the 1840s, when it was sold to the Long family. They began a number of repairs, including the hall roof, a project on which the writer Thomas Hardy's father was engaged. The Cooke family, the present owners, acquired the house in the 1960s and have carried out a number of sensitive alterations and restorations.

The principal glory of the great hall is the roof, the beams of which form a succession of arches. It dates from about 1500. The bay window, with its Perpendicular mouldings and tracery, has original stained glass depicting the heraldic emblems of the various families associated with the house – Martyn, de Mohun, de Pydele, de Loundres, de Clevedon and Kelway are shown in beautiful detail. The crest in each case is that of the Martyns. 'Martin' is an old name for an ape, and the crest has an ape looking into a mirror with the motto: 'He who looks at Martyn's ape, Martyn's ape shall look at him.' The organ in the minstrel gallery is from a design by James Wyatt dated 1800. The large Flemish tapestry over the fireplace shows Samson doing sterling work cudgelling 1000 Philistines. The mirrors were made by Thomas Johnson, a rival of Chippendale.

The door in the oriel leads the visitor to the King's Ante-room, which in turn leads to the Great Chamber. A large panelled room, with a complex plaster moulded ceiling, this was the principal withdrawing room of the 16th-century house. The beautiful harpsichord was made for Queen Charlotte in 1761 by one of the renowned Kirckman family of instrument-makers. The wine cellar is appropriately spacious for someone as linked to the wine trade as was Sir William Martyn. It is approached from the King's Ante-room, through a door which was specially widened to accept the Tudor wine casks.

A 15th-century stone and oak staircase leads from the ante-room to the Yellow Closet, and on to the King's Room, so named from its use in earlier times as the place for the Manorial Court, which met in the King's name. It is a finely panelled room with an oriel window, and is now given over to the display of 19th-century porcelain and pottery. The far side of the hall gives access to the screens passage, which has an interesting carved panel showing a yule log procession – once an important part of country house Christmas ritual. The Green Parlour, which is entered from the screens passage, occupies the site of the old buttery and kitchen. At the foot of the stairs is the dining room, which has some Chippendale-style mahogany furniture and a splendid chinoiserie-style mirror, together with another mirror by Thomas Johnson.

At the top of the main staircase lies the state bedroom. The enormous, intricately carved Tudor bed, with its heavy 'cup-and-cover' posts, came from MONTACUTE HOUSE (Somerset) and belonged to Lord Curzon. A delicate spinet here is dated 1688, and the pair of walnut barley-sugar-twist chairs and accompanying stool date from Charles I's reign. The ever-present Martyn monkey crest reappears in the overmantel of the chimneypiece, linked with the unicorn of Faringdon – the crest of Sir William's first wife.

1 mile (1.5 km) east of Puddletown, on the A35 (map pages 54–5)

1851 WINE COOLER

EARLY WINDOW

MARTYN FAMILY CREST

Continued from page 63

The famous Ham Hill stone, weathered to a deep golden hue, has never looked more beautiful than in the walls of Barrington Court.

Henry Daubeney, whose family had owned the property since the 13th century and who inherited in 1508, was the last of that name to occupy the house. He financed his extravagance at Henry VIII's court by parting with his estates and in 1543 sold the house to Sir Thomas Arundell. William Clifton purchased it from Arundell in 1559 and built the house as we see it today (it used to be thought that the house was begun in about 1514, but recent investigation has proved otherwise). The Strode family added an elegant stable block in about 1670 in what was an attractive but completely contrasting style.

The house had many owners in the 19th century and was ultimately purchased in poor shape in 1907 by the recently-formed National Trust. A complete restoration was effected by Colonel A. A. Lyle from the 1920s, remaining as close as possible to the spirit of the original house.

Although today there is no family in occupation, and the rooms are used by a furniture company, the house still exudes a graceful charm. The gardens, designed by Gertrude Jekyll, are exceptional, and the moat and the high, ancient walls cast an unusual tranquillity over the scene.

In Barrington village, 5 miles (8 km)
north-east of Ilminster, off the A303
(map pages 54–5)

BELTON HOUSE   LINCOLNSHIRE

Built in 1684–8 for Sir John Brownlow (1660–97), Belton is one of the handsomest houses of its period in the country. On Brownlow's early death the house passed to his nephew, Viscount Tyrconnel, who died without issue, and then passed to Tyrconnel's sister, Lady Anne Cust. Lady Cust was the wife of Sir John Cust, Speaker of the Commons, who is shown in an impressive portrait in the entrance hall by Reynolds. Her grandson became Baron Brownlow in 1776, and the present Lord Brownlow lives here today.

The house is 'H'-shaped in plan, spaciously symmetrical, with a genteel simplicity in the tall elevations, with their long sash windows. The hipped roof is ornamented with pedimented dormer windows and topped by a sunny cupola. The house is virtually unchanged, apart from some alterations in the late 18th century by James Wyatt, notably the barrel vault of the library ceiling, and by his nephew Sir Jeffry Wyatville, who altered the staircase and the Red Drawing Room.

Belton is famous for the woodcarving which frames some of the great portraits in the house; it is in the style of Grinling Gibbons and has been claimed as the work of his own hand. The plasterwork is also spectacular, particularly the ceilings of the saloon, staircase hall and chapel, where putti romp amid garlands of flowers. The chapel is in a sumptuous Baroque style and has a painting of the *Entombment* by Tintoretto.

Notable novelties in other rooms include a floor painted with the Brownlow arms in the Tyrconnel Room – one of the rare survivals of the custom of painting bare boards – and the pretty Chinese Bedroom, which has an exceptionally fine Chinese painted wallpaper and a late Regency half-tester bed with an ornately fringed pelmet. There is a particularly happy atmosphere in the rooms of Belton, and some very amusing stories connected with them. One of these is the tale of how, in the days when tea drinking was an exclusive luxury, Sir John Brownlow's five daughters were discovered engaging in a forbidden tea party on the first

The entrance front of Belton House

floor. They heard their mother's footsteps approaching and, in their panic to remove the evidence, threw the entire tea set – kettle, tea cloth and all – out of the window.

3 miles (5 km) north-east of Grantham,
on the A607 (map page 55)

———————◆———————

BELVOIR CASTLE   LEICESTERSHIRE

Belvoir (pronounced 'Beaver') Castle was built by James Wyatt between 1801 and 1816. The small stronghold that had previously existed on this impressive hilltop site had passed to the Manners family by a marriage in the Tudor period. Wyatt's grand new mansion was intended to reflect the rise of the family to the earldom and dukedom of Rutland. Wyatt created a vast theatrical fortress of battlements and towers in his neo-Gothic style. A disastrous fire destroyed some of his work (and a quantity of fine paintings) in 1816, but with the assistance of Wyatt's three sons, following his death, and the chaplain Sir John Thoroton, the house was eventually completed.

The Grand Staircase leads to the Gothic Ballroom, where portraits by Reynolds, Hoppner and Laura Knight may be seen. The Regent's Gallery, which is 130 ft (40 m) long, remains as Wyatt devised it and is lined with Gobelin tapestries given by the future Louis XVI in 1770, before the castle was built, and depicting the *Adventures of Don Quixote*. Two portraits by Reynolds – those of the 4th Duke and the Marquess of Granby – hang in the Grand Dining Room, which also contains Regency furniture and a large silver collection. The table in this room by Matthew Cotes Wyatt cleverly simulates a draped tablecloth but is actually made from marble. The picture gallery contains many treasures including the state bed from the Borghese Palace in Rome, some 16th-century silver and a collection of miniatures. Easily the most famous and important pictures here, however, are five canvases by Nicolas Poussin from a series representing the *Seven Sacraments* (one has been destroyed and the other survivor is in the National Gallery in Washington). Poussin was the greatest French painter of the 17th century and these are among his finest works still in private ownership.

The Chinese Bedroom, with its 18th-century, hand-painted wallpaper, leads to the Elizabethan Saloon. Here the 5th Duchess is commemorated by a regal statue sculpted by Matthew Cotes Wyatt. The opulent Louis XVI revival style of this room, with its brilliant Aubusson carpet and scintillating rose-red upholstery, started a fashion. The ceiling shows the Duke and Duchess with their four children amid allegorical figures – a fine example of the richness of late Regency taste.

6 miles (9.5 km) west of Grantham,
between the A52 and A607
(map page 55)

———————◆———————

BERRINGTON HALL   HEREFORD AND WORCESTER

Berrington Hall, built for Thomas Harley between 1775 and 1781, is a gem of a house, with a serenely beautiful exterior and some of the most exquisitely decorated interiors of the time. Harley was an acquaintance of 'Capability' Brown, and, on Brown's advice, the house was positioned on a perfect site.

Brown went on to design the excellent park, while his son-in-law Henry Holland was engaged to build the house. Holland was well on the way to becoming one of the principal architects of the day, and was a favourite of the Prince Regent, for whom he built the Pavilion at Brighton (later remodelled by Nash) and Carlton House in London. Berrington's chief glory is the series of rooms which Holland created, including the dramatic entrance hall, which is the epitome of late 18th-century taste.

The drawing room has a fine neo-classical ceiling with painted roundels attributed to Biagio Rebecca (1735–1806), a decorative painter of Italian extraction. The room has furniture from the renowned Elmer Digby collection, given to the National Trust in 1981. The collection is mostly of French pieces, several of which belonged to the Comte de

Built to honour the 1st Duke of Marlborough's victory in 1704, Blenheim Palace is a remarkable tribute to a great man

Flahaut (1785–1870), the illegitimate son of Louis XVI's minister Talleyrand. Further pieces are on view in the boudoir, which is ornamented with a fan-shaped semi-dome behind a screen. There are interesting bedrooms on display, and a nursery complete with a wide range of Victorian toys and dolls. The library has another exceptional ceiling with neo-classical paintings attributed to Rebecca.

3 miles (5 km) north of Leominster,
west of the A49 (map pages 54–5)

BLENHEIM PALACE OXFORDSHIRE

Blenheim Palace is a monument rather than a house, and was built to celebrate the great victory over Louis XIV by John Churchill, 1st Duke of Marlborough, at the Battle of Blenheim in 1704. The estate at Woodstock and the funds to build a palace on it were the gift of Queen Anne. Marlborough himself chose the architect, Sir John Vanbrugh, who was assisted, as he had been at his first great house, CASTLE HOWARD (North Yorkshire), by Nicholas Hawksmoor.

The creation of Blenheim Palace was caught up in the tempestuous politics of the day. When it was begun in 1705, the Duchess of Marlborough was a close personal friend of the Queen, but by 1720 they were at loggerheads. As the generous offer of a palace had never been confirmed in writing, Anne brought payments to an abrupt halt, and the Marlboroughs had to finance the remainder of the project themselves. In addition to their political troubles, Vanbrugh, whose architectural vision was vast and overwhelmingly extravagant, clashed continually with the Duchess, who was relentless in seeking economies, and he stormed out in a rage in 1716. Hawksmoor completed the palace in 1725, three years after the Duke of Marlborough's death.

Despite all the troubles surrounding its erection, Blenheim is the greatest Baroque residence of the country. Its rooms are richer, grander and more dramatic than any others. Vanbrugh's loftiness of vision is the key to its success, and the great portico at the entrance with the vast hall beyond (in the ceiling of which Marlborough is shown demonstrating the battle plan at Blenheim) is as magnificent a tribute to a great general as can be imagined. The picture gallery – today the library – is presided over by a life-size statue of Queen Anne, by Rysbrack. Thornhill and Laguerre painted the ceilings in the great hall and saloon respectively, and many of the great talents of the period are represented in paintings and furniture.

Sir Winston Churchill, a direct descendant of the 1st Duke of Marlborough, had a close association with Blenheim and there is an interesting exhibition of possessions and mementoes from his political career in the room in which he was born.

At the south-west end of the village of
Woodstock, 8 miles (13 km) north of
Oxford, on the A34 (map page 55)

BLICKLING HALL NORFOLK

A large, extremely handsome Jacobean house crowned with Dutch gables and an ornate clock tower, Blickling Hall was designed by Robert Lyminge, who had worked for Robert Cecil at HATFIELD HOUSE (Hertfordshire). Building began in 1616 for Sir Henry Hobart, James I's Lord

The red-brick Jacobean exterior of Blickling Hall

Chief Justice. The house remained in the Hobart family, who became the Earls of Buckinghamshire, until 1793, when it passed through the female line to the Marquesses of Lothian. The 11th Marquess left the house to the National Trust in 1940, setting an important precedent for the rescue of large country houses.

The long gallery, which stretches 123 ft (37 m), is the most celebrated room at Blickling. Its fine Jacobean plaster-work includes panels showing coats of arms and other heraldic devices, together with symbols of the Five Senses and Learning. The large library is mostly 18th-century, while the bookcases with their painted decorations were created by John Hungerford Pollen when the room was altered along Gothic Revival lines in 1860.

The Peter the Great Room was designed especially to house a gigantic tapestry showing Peter the Great defeating the Swedes at Poltava. It was woven in St Petersburg and was given by Catherine the Great to the 2nd Earl of Buckinghamshire while he was ambassador to the Russian court. Also in this room are portraits of the Earl and his wife by Gainsborough and an equestrian portrait of George II.

The adjoining state bedroom, which is coloured white and gold, has a bed dressed with crimson silk which began as a state canopy for George II. The 2nd Earl acquired it on the monarch's death. Daniel Mytens' portrait of the 1st Baronet, the builder of Blickling, hangs here together with some contemporary copies of Van Dyck's famous portraits of Charles I and Henrietta Maria. The large Axminster carpet was woven specially for this room in 1779.

The house is full of fine period furniture, most of it English, and the Chinese Bedroom, which is hung with hand-painted paper, has a painted Chinese wardrobe similar to one made by Chippendale for the actor David Garrick. One of the highlights of the diverse painting collection is a charming view of Chelsea by Canaletto.

In the village of Blickling, 1 mile (1.5 km)
north-west of Aylsham, on the B1354
(map page 55)

BOUGHTON HOUSE NORTHAMPTONSHIRE

Boughton is built around the core of an early Tudor house, but most of what the visitor sees belongs to the 1680s and 1690s. At this time the house was rebuilt for Ralph, 3rd Lord Montagu. He had been the British ambassador in Paris and his house is more strongly French in style than anything else of the date in English architecture – it has been described as a 'miniature Versailles'. Lord Montagu is known to have employed a Frenchman to rebuild his London home (now destroyed) and the same man may well have been responsible for Boughton.

A succession of wealthy wives allowed Ralph Montagu to fill his sophisticated house with treasures, and to be unstinting in the money he lavished on it. His determination to recast the old house he inherited showed itself in his masking of the hammer-beam roof of the great hall with a barrel vault. This was then decorated by the French painter Louis Chéron with a depiction of *The Marriage of Hercules and Hebe*. Montagu's taste for the very best Continental furnishings is seen, for example, in the *pier glasses* (tall, narrow wall mirrors) by the Dutch- or Flemish-born Gerreit Jensen, and in numerous pieces of French furniture. English makers include William Kent and Matthias Lock. The paintings are similarly of high quality, among the most remarkable being the collection of 40 grisaille sketches by Van Dyck.

At the end of the 18th century the estate passed by marriage to the Buccleuch family, and although maintained in good order, Boughton was little used in the 19th century. As a result, Ralph Montagu's exceptional treasure house has passed into our times little changed.

3 miles (5 km) north of Kettering, on
the A43 (map page 55)

BROADLANDS HAMPSHIRE

A combination of architectural beauty, historical interest and romantic personal association makes a visit to Broadlands a rewarding experience. The house was built for Henry Temple, 1st Viscount Palmerston, in 1736. He employed William Kent to change the course of the River Test, which flows picturesquely through the gardens in front of the house, and his son, in 1767, commissioned 'Capability' Brown to work on the garden and reconstruct the house. Brown's son-in-law Henry Holland finished the building, his work including the east portico and sculpture hall. He also undertook the decoration of the state rooms in a style derived from Robert Adam.

The sculpture hall displays impressive Greek and Roman statues, together with some 18th-century sculpture collected by the 2nd Viscount Palmerston on his Grand Tour in 1765. The Wedgwood Room, named after its collection of jasper-ware, has four Lely portraits of beauties at the court of Charles II. The drawing room and the saloon contain some fine portraits and elegant pieces of satinwood and Adam-style furniture.

The most distinguished inhabitant of Broadlands in the 19th century was the 3rd Viscount Palmerston (1784–1865), who was twice Prime Minister and three times Foreign Secretary, and in the 20th century the house passed to Edwina, wife of the 1st Earl Mountbatten of Burma. The personalities of this adventurous couple pervade the house today. In the forefront of world events throughout his distinguished career, Lord Mountbatten earned admiration and friendship all over the globe. The exhibition mounted in the stable block, opened by the Prince of Wales after Lord Mountbatten's death in 1979, gives a fascinating glimpse into the great man's life. The house is now the home of his grandson, Lord Romsey.

1 mile (1.5 km) south of Romsey, off
the A31 (map page 55)

◆

BROUGHTON CASTLE OXFORDSHIRE

It is hard to imagine a more beautiful medieval manor house than Broughton, surrounded by its pretty gardens and a wide moat, in which the water seems to move as slowly as time has in the house. Remodelled in the 16th century

Broughton Castle, built as a fortified manor house

in the Tudor style, the house retains much of its earlier, 14th-century structure (it was perhaps begun by Sir John de Broughton, who died in 1315); the most interesting survival is the chapel, which dates from the 1330s and is largely unaltered.

Since the mid 15th century Broughton has belonged to the family of the present owner, Lord Saye and Sele. In the 17th century, the 1st Viscount Saye and Sele helped plot the downfall of Charles I at secret meetings held in the house's council chamber. A portrait of this aristocratic agitator, who was known as 'Old Subtlety', hangs in the vaulted dining room against the fine linenfold panelling. The great hall dates from the 14th century, but has broad 16th-century windows and a Tudor plaster ceiling, which may have been further gothicized by Sanderson Miller in the 1760s. The gallery contains a pair of marble busts by Rysbrack, one of Inigo Jones, the other of Ben Jonson.

The Oak Room has exceptional late 16th-century oak carving, and a rare internal porch surmounted by a Latin motto in a cartouche which says: 'There is no pleasure in the memory of the past.' There is little pleasure in the memory of William Thomas, 15th Baron Saye and Sele, a dandy whose heady pursuit of pleasure at the Regency court resulted in the house running into neglect and a great sale of all the contents, down to the last swan from the moat. In the 1860s and 1870s, however, Frederick, 16th Baron,

71

The medieval buildings of Brympton d'Evercy, set amid vineyard and garden

consulted the architect Sir George Gilbert Scott on a complete and sensitive restoration, which saved this lovely house for the future.

In the village of Broughton, 3 miles
(5 km) south-west of Banbury, on the
B4035 (map page 55)

◆

BRYMPTON D'EVERCY SOMERSET

The house and its outbuildings stand next to the church and collectively they form one of the most beautiful ensembles of medieval buildings in England, particularly as the local honey-coloured Ham Hill stone is so pleasing to the eye. The church, with its curious belfry, blends with the medieval priest's house, which links with the main façade, where large leaded windows flank a whimsical Georgian 'Gothick' porch. The original Tudor porch is to the left, and houses the oldest external working clock in the country. The church and the priest's house date from the 13th to the 15th century, when the d'Evercys lived here, and the church contains the effigy of the priest who served the house during the Black Death. The house itself dates from the 1520s and was built by the Sydenham family.

The long south front is a charmingly rustic piece of early classicism dating from 1678, built by the rather peculiarly named Sir John Posthumous Sydenham. It is an asymmetrical composition of segmental and triangular pediments, and where there would normally be a central focal feature in such a classical scheme, here there is only a drainpipe.

The Sydenhams had always lived well beyond their means and ultimately, in 1731, the house was sold to Francis Fane. The house is still occupied by his family, who through a number of good 19th-century marriages acquired the name of Clive-Ponsonby-Fane. The present owners have restored a great deal of the house's domestic character and comfortable charm. Wine is made from grapes growing in the garden, and the combination of such a romantic ensemble of unaltered buildings and a vineyard is extremely picturesque.

2 miles (3 km) west of Yeovil, off the
A30 or A3088 (map pages 54–5)

◆

BURGHLEY HOUSE CAMBRIDGESHIRE

From a distance, Burghley, with its riot of towers, spires, chimneys and finials, looks less like a house than a small town. One of the biggest and most lavish of private palaces of the 16th century, it was built in 1566–87 for William Cecil, 1st Lord Burghley, right-hand-man to Elizabeth I. The wealth and rank that Cecil created has lasted to the present day, and the house is still occupied by his descendants.

The exterior of the house has remained unaltered, but there have been many changes inside, notably the creation of a suite of apartments known as the George Rooms in 1681–1700. These contain some of the most ambitious decorative painting in the country, mainly by Antonio Verrio, an Italian-born artist who settled in England in about 1671. He was hugely successful and made a fortune, but anyone who has seen good examples of Continental mural painting of the period will realize that his talents fell somewhat short of his European rivals. His most famous work at Burghley is in the saloon, known as the 'Heaven Room'. The Olympian gods are crowding together to witness the embarrassment of Venus and Mars, caught in adulterous lovemaking by Vulcan. Verrio could not resist the temptation to paint himself amid the gods, and he is easy to spot to the left of the forge, draped in a brown cloak.

Further architectural additions were made from 1756 to 1783 for the 9th Earl by 'Capability' Brown. Brown worked around the 17th-century rooms in a tactful way, ensuring that his classical rooms complemented rather than upstaged the earlier suites.

The house contains several portraits of Burghley and Elizabeth I, and many later portraits by artists such as Kneller, Lely, Gainsborough and Lawrence. Among the

73

masterpieces of furniture are some outstandingly good Chippendale commodes and, particularly apt for so large a house, a Queen Anne wine cooler which is said to be the largest in the world.

In a large park on the south-east side
of Stamford, near the A1
(map page 55)

◆

Burton Constable Humberside

The Constable family have owned Burton Constable since the 12th century. The present house was built in about 1570–1600 and remodelled by William Constable between 1750 and 1770 with advice from 'Capability' Brown, James Wyatt, Thomas Atkinson and John Carr of York. Thomas Lightholer was responsible for the great hall and the staircase hall, with its beautiful balustrade, whereas Atkinson created the billiard room (now the chapel) and Wyatt designed the Great Drawing Room. Chippendale supplied furniture for this sumptuous room, and his 16 gilt armchairs are particularly graceful. This room also contains fine Dutch and Flemish paintings of the 17th and 18th centuries.

For a house which had such a wealth of talent lavished upon it from so many different sources, the style is remarkably coherent and consistent. William Constable's excellent taste is largely responsible for this, and his reliance on the best local craftsmen is admirable, in an age often blinded by the glories and glamour of the capital. Furniture by Lowry, the estate carpenter, and building by Henderson of York both compare well with the work of the more famous designers.

William Constable was not just a patron of the arts, but also a gifted scientist with a broad interest in geology, physics and zoology. His exceptional mind was usually employed on experiments with electricity or vacuums – anything which seemed to push back the frontiers of knowledge. These experiments took place in the long gallery, which Constable referred to as his 'Philosophical Room', but his equipment and books are now displayed in the museum rooms.

Near the village of Sproatley, 7 miles
(11 km) north-east of Hull, on the
B1238 (map page 56)

◆

Calke Abbey Derbyshire

When Calke Abbey was first opened to the public in April 1989, it was hailed as 'a house trapped in time', and it is certainly one of the most extraordinary houses open to the public in Britain.

From 1701 to 1704 the Harpur family encased their Tudor house in a Baroque skin. No architect is recorded as having worked at Calke, and the planning and detailing of the house are surprisingly casual. The lack of professional involvement is reflected in the comment about Calke by Elizabeth Coke of nearby Melbourne Hall that 'the thing is done but nobody did it'.

This lack of concern with fashionable convention was quite in keeping with the Harpur family, and the 'timelessness' of the house today is a direct product of what was tactfully called their 'unsociability'. Having never really made an impact among the local aristocracy, the Harpurs and Harpur-Crewes (as they became in 1808) developed into virtual recluses. In 1789, Sir Henry Harpur, the 'isolated baronet', inherited the house and from that day the house entered into a curious state of limbo. Possessions accumulated, and under the influence of Sir Vauncey Harpur-Crewe (1846–1924) the house began to fill up with a host of natural history specimens. As rooms filled and were left, the 20th century progressed unnoticed and unwelcomed; the few visitors were still ferried to and from the park gates by horse and cart.

In 1985 the National Trust acquired the house and had the exacting, but exciting, task of sifting the two centuries of clutter. They found that Calke had some extraordinary treasures. A harpsichord by the Swiss-born master Burkat Shudi was pulled from a loft, a music manuscript by Haydn

Continued on page 78

The grand front of Calke Abbey – 'a house trapped in time'

Guided Tour

CASTELL COCH SOUTH GLAMORGAN

Castell Coch is an extravagant and whimsical house. Built between 1871 and 1891, it was the personal dream of the 3rd Marquis of Bute in partnership with the architect William Burges. Their intention was to take the picturesque ruins of the medieval castle and turn them into a palace 'fit for a Sleeping Beauty'. The result was romantic, eccentric, and strangely haunting.

Burges' Gothic style was heavily influenced by the romantic medievalism of the Pre-Raphaelite movement, and although he was highly knowledgeable about medieval architecture, he created a fantasy vision of the Middle Ages rather than an archaeologically exact one. He included turrets, drawbridges, arrow-slits, portcullises and other warlike features, but they endow the castle with a toy-like rather than a threatening appearance. He also designed the furnishings and decorative elements of the interior.

Standing in dense beech woods, overlooking the River Taff, its pointed turrets just visible above the leaves, Castell Coch occupies an appropriately romantic site. It consists of three massive circular towers surrounding an open court, and is approached by a short drawbridge. Inside, every surface is painted in high Pre-Raphaelite style, rich with imagery and gaudy beauty. The hall is entered by a covered wooden stair and its lofty roof is decorated with stencilled patterns; the chimney breast supports a statue of St Lucius, a mythical early king of England.

The keep – the largest of the three towers – contains the magnificent drawing room. Burges originally planned two rooms, but then combined them to make a soaring space, surrounded by a high balcony rising to cusped arches and a ribbed vault. The room is spectacularly painted on a theme of *Life and Death in Nature*. The lower level shows scenes from Aesop's *Fables*, and rabbits, cats, frogs and mice sit in gracious postures amid the vegetation. The panels develop into 58 different floral designs as they rise up the walls. The stonework incorporates animals and insects, many of which are painted, and the ribs of the vault are studded with butterflies. The vault itself rises to a starry sky populated by a flock of exotic birds. Above the fireplace is a sculptured composition of the Three Fates, daughters of Zeus, spinning the destiny of mankind. The rope they each hold, and which loops between them, symbolizes life. Clotho, on the left, spins the thread of life, Lachesis measures its length, and Atropos cuts it at death.

Above the drawing room, and approached by a narrow spiral staircase, lies the second principal room of the house – Lady Bute's bedroom. An arcade of shallow arches encircles the room, and on the hooded chimneypiece is a figure of Psyche – represented as a human butterfly. The domed ceiling is panelled in

CHIMNEYPIECE

WINGED FIGURE OF PSYCHE

CEILING VAULT

Castell Coch, the romantic 'castle in the air', surrounded by beech woods

mirror glass and painted designs of brambles and thorns.

The furniture is extraordinary and ranges from the washstand with its twin castellated towers to the richly painted cupboard and chairs. Lying in the centre of the room is the huge square bed, painted and gilded in rich colours; it is surmounted by eight clear crystal balls from which sparks of light scatter over the painted walls.

Equal care was lavished on Lord Bute's bedroom, and this room also sports some interesting, though uncomfortable-looking, furniture. The stencilling is exceptional, forming intricate geometrical patterns on the walls and ceiling. The carving on the frieze of the chimneypiece shows a range of little animals appearing among ivy and brambles. The window towards the courtyard opens on to a romantic balcony with views of turrets and weathervanes beyond.

Castell Coch was finally completed in 1891. Ironically it was never really used. Bute preferred to be engaged in ongoing projects, and took little interest in his completed masterpiece. The Bute children occupied the house during periods of 'quarantine' when poorly with infectious illnesses, but Bute's death in 1900 sealed the fate of Castell Coch as a lavish and painstakingly perfect folly.

5 miles (8 km) north-west of Cardiff, off the A470, near the village of Tongwynlais (map page 54)

Continued from page 74

was discovered under layers of dust, and the stables held a number of complete 18th- and 19th-century carriages. Chief among all the treasures, however, is the state bed, which was the wedding gift of Princess Anne (daughter of George II) to the wife of Sir Henry Harpur, 5th Baronet, in 1734. Left unopened in their packing cases for over two centuries, the embroidered Chinese hangings are as fresh and vibrant as the day they were sewn.

4 miles (6.5 km) north of Ashby de la
Zouch, south of the A514, between the
B5006 and the B587 (map page 55)

◆

CASTLE HOWARD   NORTH YORKSHIRE

The view of Castle Howard from across the lake is one of the most famous of all country house vistas. The dramatic silhouette, massive yet elegant, seems to typify the grandeur of ducal living. This is not just a modern reaction, for contemporaries beheld the house with equal awe and excitement, as indicated by Horace Walpole's famous remark: 'I have seen gigantic palaces before, but never a sublime one.'

It was built for Charles Howard, 3rd Earl of Carlisle, Earl Marshal of England, to replace the family home at Henderskelfe Castle, which burned down in 1693. He had the courage to choose as his designer Sir John Vanbrugh, a soldier turned playwright who, as far as is known, had no previous architectural experience. Nicholas Hawksmoor was Vanbrugh's assistant, and, with his long training under Wren, no doubt ironed out some of Vanbrugh's rough edges. What Vanbrugh did have was vision, and he set about the project with gusto. It proved to be a long task – by 1738 (12 years after Vanbrugh's death) only the central block and east wing were erected. In the 1750s there followed the rather different Palladian-style west block designed by Sir Thomas Robinson. Castle Howard, as a result, is somewhat lop-sided and is symmetrical only on its rear elevation.

The immense great hall is the most splendid room in the house and is capped by a dome – a new feature in English domestic architecture. It was decorated with frescoes by the Venetian painter Giovanni Antonio Pellegrini, but these were destroyed by fire in 1940 and have been replaced with copies.

Other rooms are filled with treasures which testify to the family's enduring position in the world as patrons and collectors. Holbein's portraits of Henry VIII and the 3rd Duke of Norfolk together with portraits by Van Dyck, Lely, Kneller, Lawrence and Opie grace the long gallery, and fine Meissen, Crown Derby and Chelsea china abounds; of particular note is the Hans Sloane Botanical Service. There is also a large and varied costume museum. The gardens and grounds are beautiful and contain exceptional buildings by Hawksmoor, who designed a huge and powerful mausoleum, and Vanbrugh.

5 miles (8 km) west of Malton, off the
A64 (map page 56)

◆

CHARLECOTE PARK   WARWICKSHIRE

Although originally an Elizabethan house, Charlecote is an excellent example of the Victorians' ability to enlarge and 'improve' an old house to make an almost completely new building. At the heart of Charlecote is the house built by Sir Thomas Lucy in about 1558. Here Elizabeth I was entertained at breakfast in 1572, and here – according to popular legend – the young William Shakespeare (a native of nearby Stratford-upon-Avon) was arraigned by Sir Thomas for poaching. The gatehouse on the door of which he is said to have pinned ribald verses about Sir Thomas has survived, but the remainder of the Tudor building was lost to George Hammond Lucy's alterations between 1825 and 1850.

The great hall, altered in 1833, retains its original heraldic glass, weapons and antlers. Among the portraits are works by Richardson and Gainsborough, and there are busts of Elizabeth I, Shakespeare and George Hammond Lucy and his wife. The large table in the centre was made for the eccentric patron William Beckford for his Gothic fantasy

The south front of Castle Howard, viewed from the great parterre

79

Charlecote Park, heavily restored in Victorian times

home Fonthill Abbey in Wiltshire (now destroyed) and was bought by George Hammond Lucy in 1823. Also from Fonthill is an exotic ebony bed made from a 17th-century East Indian settee.

The dining room and library are true mid-Victorian examples of taste, with bold wallpapers in rich colours. The library has a rare silver-gilt Tudor wine cup of 1524, and the dining room holds the 'Charlecote Buffet', a huge and impressive, if rather ungainly, piece of carved furniture, declined as a gift by Queen Victoria. Mrs George Hammond Lucy, who acquired it, described it as 'throbbing with life'. The tapestry room has ebony and ivory furniture of the Restoration period, probably of Indian origin. The drawing room contains a pair of Chinese Chippendale rococo pier glasses.

The outbuildings at Charlecote are perfectly preserved and display the workings of a country house as they appeared in the last century. The brewhouse and kitchen are particularly interesting – and these areas must once have been particularly busy: in 1845 there were 4000 gallons of ale stored in the cellars under the house.

4 miles (6.5 km) east of Stratford-upon-Avon, off the B4086 (map page 55)

CHATSWORTH DERBYSHIRE

Chatsworth reaches a scale of grandeur and magnificence achieved by very few private houses. The landscape, in which everything has been worked, shaped, planted and improved, provides the perfect backdrop to the house, which sits at the bottom of a beautiful valley, surrounded by its ordered gardens.

The house was begun in 1552 by Sir William Cavendish and his wife Elizabeth ('Bess of Hardwick'), built around a central courtyard. One of their sons became the 1st Earl of Devonshire, and his descendant, the 1st Duke of Devonshire, set about reconstructing the now old-fashioned house in Baroque style between 1687 and 1707. William Talman was the architect of the impressive south front (1687–96), the first convincingly Baroque façade in England. However, the remainder was tackled in a piecemeal way, working on each side of the square separately. Not only were the façades built at different times, but different architects were responsible for them, a situation caused partly by feuds over payment and quarrels over design. The peculiarity of the building was exaggerated by the work of the 6th Duke, for whom Sir Jeffry Wyatville added a long north wing surmounted by a tower in the 1830s.

The Baroque state rooms, painted by Verrio and Laguerre, begin with the huge painted hall. Under the great stair, with its ornate balustrade by Jean Tijou (the greatest ironworker of his day), stands one of the most delightful items in Chatsworth, a baby carriage designed by William Kent. It is formed from a classical shell resting on writhing snakes and has two long serpents (taken from the Cavendish coat of arms) as the harness for the goat that once pulled it.

The state apartments on the top floor replaced the Elizabethan long gallery, and form a perfect example of the Baroque *enfilade* system of interconnecting rooms, in which the doors form a sequence through which a long vista is obtained. Verrio painted the ceiling in the state dining room (look out for Mrs Hackett, the much disliked housekeeper, portrayed as one of the Three Fates, cutting the thread of life, to the left of the chimneypiece). The enormous table

Right Chatsworth, set in magnificent surroundings

in this room is by William Kent. The mirror at the end of the room, which stands in a door surround, was added to give the impression that the *enfilade* of apartments continues for the same distance in the opposite direction.

Chatsworth has one of the finest collections of paintings to be found in any country house, including works by distinguished foreign artists (above all Rembrandt) as well as by a succession of great British portraitists. The collection is unusual in including important contemporary art – a group of paintings by Lucien Freud, grandson of Sigmund Freud and one of the most powerful and individual British artists of the present day. Also at Chatsworth is one of the best private collections of Old Master drawings in the world, but this is not open to the public.

4 miles (6.5 km) east of Bakewell,
7 miles (11 km) west of Chesterfield,
off the A619 (map pages 55–6)

◆

CHICHELEY HALL   BUCKINGHAMSHIRE

Chicheley is a house of great character. Built of red brick from 1720 to 1725, and of unusual Baroque design, it is attributed to the architect Francis Smith of Warwick. The façades are curiously 'curvy', with bold cornices which sweep up to a projecting central bay (slicing through windows in the process). Corinthian pilasters ornament all sides, augmented in the middle section by flamboyant arched window architraves. The pediment over the entrance is unusually extravagant, and it is said to show signs of Austrian influence.

Inside, the rooms are more Palladian than Baroque, with a beautifully proportioned entrance hall containing an elegant marble-columned screen by Henry Flitcroft, and a ceiling painting by William Kent. The staircase is in oak with bands of inlaid walnut, and has finely-turned balusters in groups of three different designs per tread. The woodwork throughout the house is of the highest quality,

Left The view up the drive towards Chicheley Hall

and the panelling, especially in the drawing and dining rooms, is especially noteworthy. Richly moulded doorframes, pilasters and cornices – carved in walnut and embellished with gold leaf – complement the swags of fruit and flowers.

The house was built by Sir John Chester, and remained in the possession of the Chester family for some 300 years. In 1952 Chicheley was acquired by the 2nd Earl Beatty, and the house contains many mementoes of his father's career as one of the great admirals of World War I. One of the more unusual of these is the bronze lion which Beatty placed on the desk in front of the German commander at the surrender of the German fleet in 1918.

In Lord Beatty's Study is his portrait by John Singer Sargent, and a portrait of Nelson by L. F. Abbott (one of numerous versions), in addition to naval scenes and seascapes. Sir John Chester's Library, reached by the back staircase, has fine panelling which cleverly conceals the bookshelves behind. Only the hinges suggest that in this room all is not what it seems.

2 miles (3 km) north-east of Newport
Pagnell, on the A422 (map page 55)

◆

CHISWICK HOUSE   LONDON

Although Chiswick House is now surrounded by suburban West London, it was built as a rural retreat in 1725–9, originally as an annexe to an Elizabethan house which has since been demolished. Its creator, the 3rd Earl Burlington, was the leader of the Palladian movement in England. He was a highly talented amateur architect and the design of the house is his own, although the interior decoration is by his protégé, William Kent. It was not built as a dwelling, but as a place of recreation and entertainment, where Burlington and his friends could enjoy the pleasures of conversation, reading and viewing his art treasures.

The building was inspired by Palladio's famous 'Villa Rotunda' near Vicenza, with the rooms radiating from a central octagon in a variety of unusual and pleasing shapes.

The statue of Palladio at the foot of the entrance stair at Chiswick House

The central domed area, with its coffered ceiling and four grand doorways, is like an artistic shrine, and it is easy to imagine the poet Alexander Pope, with Kent and Burlington, discussing some point of classical taste or learning here.

Unfortunately, the superb furniture made by Kent for the building is now at CHATSWORTH (Derbyshire) and the rooms are not seen as they were intended. The garden, however, is filled with temples, fountains and sculpture and is largely unchanged. It holds an important place in the history of garden design, leading the way towards the 'natural' landscapes of 'Capability' Brown later in the century.

In Burlington Lane, Chiswick
(map page 55)

CLAYDON HOUSE   BUCKINGHAMSHIRE

The fairly simple 18th-century façade of Claydon was added to an older red-brick house by the 2nd Earl Verney in 1754–65. He sank all his wealth and abundant taste into the house until he was bankrupt. However, on his death, his successor promptly demolished two thirds of the enormous building he had erected and now only the west wing of the original house remains. The austerity of the façade conceals a suite of rococo rooms of rare extravagance.

The Chinese Room on the first floor is the greatest achievement of the chinoiserie style in Britain. One whole wall is a make-believe pagoda, with little bells hanging from the eaves. The doors are rich with scrolls and pagoda roofs, and the faces of little Chinamen peep out from rocky ledges and fretwork fencing. This virtuoso woodwork is by an otherwise unknown Mr Lightfoot, whose talent was clearly considerable. Further evidence of Lightfoot's skill can be seen in the Pink Parlour, North Hall and Upper Gothic Room, and in the richly carved wood ceiling over the main staircase. The staircase is inlaid with ebony and ivory in geometrical patterns and is ornamented with a delicate balustrade of wheat ears that tremble naturalistically with the step of each passer-by.

In addition to fine furniture and paintings, the house displays mementoes of Florence Nightingale, who retired to Claydon House after her nursing career was over to live with her elder sister Parthenope, who married Sir Harry Verney in 1858.

In the village of Middle Claydon,
4 miles (6.5 km) south-west of Winslow,
off the A413 (map page 55)

CORSHAM COURT   WILTSHIRE

Anticipating the inheritance of an outstanding art collection, the owner of Corsham, Paul Methuen, commissioned 'Capability' Brown in 1745 to enlarge and improve the old Tudor house. The rooms Brown designed form a magnificent ensemble and create a fitting setting for one of the most imposing private art galleries in the country. The picture gallery itself, a triple cube (that is, three times as long as it is high and wide) hung with its original crimson damask and with a sophisticated stucco ceiling, has exceptional sofas and chairs attributed to Thomas Chippendale. The fireplace is the work of the sculptor Peter Scheemakers and on it stands a bust of the collector of the paintings, Sir

The Tudor building of Corsham Court was modified in 1745

Paul Methuen (cousin of the Paul Methuen who was responsible for the improvements). The collection is particularly notable for 17th-century Italian paintings, and Van Dyck is also well represented.

The Cabinet Room contains some splendid *pietre dure* cabinets (*pietre dure* is an Italian term for hard or semiprecious stones carved decoratively), and a Fra Filippo Lippi *Annunciation*, painted *c.* 1463 for the Cathedral of Pistoia, hangs in this room. The exceptionally fine ensemble of commode, torchères and pier glasses dates from 1772 and is all, apart from the mirror by Robert Adam, by John Cobb. Cobb supplied furniture to Buckingham House (now Palace) at about this time. His inlay work on these particular pieces sums up the superb quality associated with the furnishings and fittings at Corsham.

In the town of Corsham, 4 miles
(6.5 km) south-west of Chippenham,
off the A4 (map pages 54–5)

◆

COTEHELE HOUSE CORNWALL

Perched on the cliffs above the River Tamar, with dramatic views of the Tamar Bridge, Cotehele is a perfect example of the small, fortified manor house. The Edgcumbe family took possession of the house in 1353, and it was remodelled in the 15th and 16th centuries by Sir Piers Edgcumbe, son of Sir Richard, who had fought with the future Henry VII against Richard III at the Battle of Bosworth Field. Henry VII rewarded Sir Richard, and the Edgcumbes continued to prosper, eventually acquiring in the 18th century a barony, a viscountcy and finally an earldom. Fortunately, by the late 17th century, Cotehele was considered too humble for the family and they moved to a new house nearby, consigning Cotehele to use as a dower house. This meant that the house was occupied by the oldest members of the family only, and though it was maintained in good order it was never considered worthy of change or modernization.

Cotehele looks rather severe from outside – the windows are small and few, and the granite elevations are formidably strong. It was built at a time when houses were still fortified and crenellated – the arrow-slits on the entrance front were never actually used, but they reflect the dangerous times in which the Edgcumbes lived. In true medieval style, the house is built around a courtyard; as one steps inside, the atmosphere becomes instantly tranquil and protective. The courtyard walls have large mullioned windows with original leaded lights, and facing the gatehouse is the great hall, added by Sir Piers in about 1520.

The hall is unusual in that it never appears to have had a screens passage. Its open, beamed ceiling is an impressive construction, and the walls are decorated with examples of armour and weaponry of the 16th and 17th centuries. The rooms are hung with rare and important tapestries and have examples of fine 16th- and 17th-century furniture. Romantic-minded visitors will probably enjoy the secret closets hidden behind the tapestries, one of which contains a squint hole through which the hall can be viewed.

Other points of interest include the kitchen, which has a full range of 18th-century utensils together with high-backed settles and an open range, and the clock in the chapel, installed in 1489 and one of the earliest domestic clocks to have survived. The garden is full of secluded spots and surprising vistas. An ancient circular dovecote adds considerable charm to the sloping walk down to the river, through which runs a cascade from a spring-filled pond.

1 mile (1.5 km) west of Calstock,
8 miles (13 km) south-west of Tavistock,
off the A390 (map page 54)

◆

CRAGSIDE NORTHUMBERLAND

Cragside was built by Richard Norman Shaw for Sir William George Armstrong (later Baron Armstrong of Cragside) between 1870 and 1884. It perches, in Wagnerian splendour and isolation, above a picturesque valley, its battlements, gables, half-timbering and gargoyles standing out against a dense backdrop of forestry. Lord Armstrong

Cotehele House grew over two generations of the Edgcumbe family in early Tudor times

was a brilliant inventor and one of the greatest Victorian industrialists; his enormous fortune came from his engineering works at Elswick on the Tyne, particularly from hydraulic cranes and armaments. Shaw captured something of the man in the house, which is a vigorous combination of vernacular styles, without any particular regional slant, put together with inventiveness and bravado. He is said to have planned the whole house in a day, while his fellow guests on the estate were out shooting.

The interior reflects the prevailing Arts and Crafts taste. The most remarkable room is the drawing room, which was hacked from the rock and is lit from a large, dramatic recessed bay window set high above the room. It is curiously detached from the other entertaining rooms by a walkway of passages, lobbies and vestibules extending some 165 ft (50 m). The room was officially opened by the Prince and Princess of Wales in 1884, and a beautiful book of watercolours, presented by the people of nearby Rothbury, commemorates the visit. Its most striking feature is a flamboyant chimneypiece above an inglenook, carved in an intricate Renaissance style.

The library, with its heavily carved oak ceiling and colourful Pre-Raphaelite paintings (on loan from the De Morgan Foundation), has furniture made by Gillow, much of it to Shaw's design. The stained glass of the bay window was made by Morris and Co. (see page 40), who also supplied wallpapers for several bedrooms. Another unusual chimney arrangement is seen here, with a wide Gothic arch and frieze appearing above the fireplace, which also has an inglenook.

Late in life Lord Armstrong named his recreations as 'planting, building, electrical and scientific research', and Cragside is the great monument to his interests. It was the first house to be lit by hydro-electric power, with luxury features such as hydraulic lifts, hot and cold Turkish baths, and miles of underground piping. Armstrong also planted thousands of trees and shrubs, transforming a bleak hillside into a magnificent park (the rhododendrons are particularly admired). An extremely

Left Cragside's dramatic site posed problems for its builders

generous man (he was a great benefactor to his native Newcastle-upon-Tyne), Armstrong was a princely host at Cragside and many of the leading figures of the day were among his guests there.

Near the town of Rothbury, 15 miles
(24 km) north-west of Morpeth, off the
A697 and B6341 (map page 56)

CULZEAN CASTLE STRATHCLYDE

Culzean (pronounced 'Killane') Castle has a superb setting, perched on the edge of a sheer cliff looking out over 20 miles (32 km) of sea to the distant isles of Arran. In 1777 the 10th Earl Cassilis decided that the medieval tower house, from which he and his ancestors had indulged in the bloody politics of the lowlands for over 500 years, was no longer an adequate reflection of the family status, so he employed Robert Adam to rebuild the house completely. Adam responded brilliantly to the challenge, creating a romantic exterior whose details alluded to the past yet were obviously the product of the sophisticated Georgian age. Inside, Adam's work is completely of his own age and of the highest quality.

The staircase shows Adam at his most inventive – it is oval, and rises through three stories, supported by two delicate colonnades. This is a famous example of Adam breaking some of the classical rules of architecture, for he places the Ionic order above the Corinthian, contrary to the traditional practice. The principal room of the state apartments on the first floor is the saloon – a dramatic circular room placed in Adam's central tower, with views over the sea. The other rooms are exquisitely decorated in Adam style, and contain outstanding pieces of original Adam furniture. Other pieces include a pair of satinwood commodes by Charles Elliott, who was cabinet-maker to the King, and a set of six George II chairs which had covers made by the Duke of Wellington's mother. The paintings include seascapes by Willem van de Velde the Younger, one of the greatest Dutch marine painters of the 17th century. He spent much of his career in England and founded the British tradition of marine painting.

After World War II, part of the house was offered to President Eisenhower for his personal use as a symbol of national gratitude. There is a permanent exhibition of his life and achievements.

12 miles (19 km) south-west of Ayr, off
the A719 (map page 56)

◆

DORNEY COURT BUCKINGHAMSHIRE

Nestling between the town of Windsor and the M4 is the unexpectedly pretty and ancient Dorney Court. First built in 1440 in wood and brick, the house is delightfully romantic and picturesque. Ancient clipped yew hedges frame the medley of sloping gables and twinkling leaded lights which make up the entrance front of the house. Only the occasional Georgian sash window reminds us that five centuries have passed since it was first built.

The Palmer family have lived at Dorney Court since the reign of Elizabeth I, and few of them have made any changes. This is particularly evident in the great hall, complete with the medieval arrangement of a screens passage leading to the kitchen and an oriel window lighting the raised dais where the lord dined with his family (see page 12). The hall contains interesting portraits and some fine linenfold panelling brought from Faversham Abbey. Beyond the hall is the parlour – probably the oldest part of the house – and above

Dorney Court, built in 1440

this is the great chamber. Both of these rooms contain impressive pieces of furniture from a range of periods.

The first pineapple to be grown in England is said to have been grown at Dorney and was presented to Charles II in 1661. The pineapple was thereafter taken up as a symbol of the age and can frequently be seen as a finial on houses of the period.

In the village of Dorney, 3 miles (5 km)
west of Slough, on the B3020
(map page 55)

◆

DRUMLANRIG CASTLE DUMFRIES AND GALLOWAY

The land on which this dramatic house stands was given to the Douglas family by Robert the Bruce in the early 14th century, although the house we see today was created between 1679 and 1691. It is a monument of peculiar style. The basic form of the building is the traditional Scottish tower, but the splendid entrance front, with its twin curved staircases, Corinthian pilasters and pedimented windows, points firmly towards the English Baroque. The central projecting bay with its blind arch, segmental pediment and octagonal cupola is unique and surprising.

The house was built for William Douglas, 1st Duke of Queensberry, and the architect was either Robert Mylne, the King's master mason, or James Smith his son-in-law. Fine panelling and carving characterizes the princely interior, and the staircase hall boasts the earliest wooden balustraded staircase in Scotland. Now owned by the Duke of Buccleuch and Queensberry, the house contains treasures of the Montagu-Douglas-Scott families, as do his other houses Bowhill (Borders) and BOUGHTON (Northamptonshire).

Notable furniture includes a pair of Louis XIV cabinets given by Louis himself to Charles II, a pair of exceptional Queen Anne mirrors, eight William and Mary silver sconces bearing the Queen's cypher, and a magnificent silver chandelier. The painting collection is of equally outstanding quality and is crowned by a work that would grace any gallery in the world – Rembrandt's *Old Woman Reading*, painted in 1655. Even more famous than the Rembrandt, however, is Leonardo da Vinci's *Virgin of the Yarnwinder*. Some authorities think that it is from Leonardo's own hand (or from his studio), whereas others consider it an extremely good copy. There are also works by other distinguished 16th- and 17th-century Continental masters (notably Holbein, Murillo and Jacob van Ruisdael) as well as many fine family portraits by leading British artists.

18 miles (29 km) north of Dumfries, off
the A76 (map page 56)

DYRHAM PARK   AVON

Dyrham Park was built between 1692 and 1704 by William Blathwayt (*c*.1649–1717). He built a house which encapsulated the Baroque taste in architecture and the Dutch taste in furnishing – both of which were the height of their vogue at the time. An otherwise unknown French architect, S. Hauduroy, designed the west front in 1692, and William Talman, the leading country house architect in the 1690s, designed the entrance front in 1698. Between the two phases of building, Blathwayt had risen to the post of Secretary of State to William III.

Blathwayt's career took him to The Hague, and it was there that his taste for Dutch painting and blue-and-white delftware developed. Works by David Teniers the Younger, Frans Snyders and other Netherlandish masters are to be seen in the house, while the famous *trompe-l'œil* of a *View down a Corridor* by Samuel van Hoogstraeten (a pupil of Rembrandt) is in the Gilt Leather Closet. The painting is placed at the end of an *enfilade* of state rooms which stretches across the east front, and seen from a distance as it is, it cleverly conveys the effect of extending the vista, rather like a doorway into the past.

Dutch delftware is seen in the form of *tulipières* (pyramidal tulip vases), urns and plates. Tile pictures of exotic scenes can be seen in the west hall, where Cromwellian chairs are covered in Dutch leather, and where there

is also a fascinating dummy-board figure of *A Woman a-pareing* [sic] *of an Apple*. These interesting objects – life-size cut-out figures – were used as fire screens, and were also said to provide company.

Some of the outstanding furniture of the house is also Dutch – most notably the walnut dining chairs in the style of the Dutch designer Daniel Marot, seen in the great hall, and the state bed in the Queen Anne Room, which was made in 1704. It is carved and upholstered in crimson and yellow velvet, and the interior is covered in sprigged satin.

The Diogenes Room contains two Mortlake tapestries representing themes from Greek philosophy, *Alexander visiting Diogenes* and *The School of Plato*, and a fine seaweed marquetry writing table. This type of inlay often appears on walnut pieces of the late 17th and early 18th centuries. The pair of 'bookpresses' in the great hall are among the earliest examples of freestanding bookcases and are similar to those designed by Thomas Sympson for Samuel Pepys in 1666 (now in Magdalene College, Cambridge).

4 miles (6.5 km) south of Chipping
Sodbury, off the A46 (map pages 54–5)

ELTON HALL   CAMBRIDGESHIRE

Elton Hall was acquired by the Proby family in 1660 and has been their home ever since; the frequent additions have resulted in a house which has a fascinating mixture of styles. Sir Thomas Proby completed a rebuilding of the house in 1666, retaining the medieval chapel and gatehouse. In the 18th century the house took on a Gothick guise as John Proby, who was created 1st Earl of Carysfort, enlarged the house and decorated it with battlements and towers. In the early 19th century additional sham defences were constructed in wood and paint, and although these were later removed the house retains its air of romance.

Inside, splendid 18th-century rooms contrast with interesting late Victorian alterations – such as the staircase hall by Henry Ashton, which is in a crisp, delicate style. Elton has a fine collection of the work of 18th- and 19th-century

Elton Hall is made up of a mixture of styles

British artists, including Gainsborough, Constable, Millais and Alma-Tadema. There is also one of the nation's principal private libraries, which holds, among many other treasures, the prayer book of Henry VIII, in which can be seen the handwriting of two of his wives.

The dining room straddles the old boundary between Cambridgeshire and Huntingdonshire, leading to the delightful claim that the lord of the house and his wife dined in different counties.

In the village of Elton, 5 miles (8 km)
south-west of Peterborough, on the
A605 (map page 55)

ERDDIG CLWYD

There is something about Erddig (pronounced 'Earthig') which makes it impossible to forget. It is not just a treasure house of beautiful paintings, furniture and silver, but a detailed microcosm of life in the 18th century. No other house in Britain conjures up so vividly the extremes of difference between the saw-pit and the saloon, the laundry and the library.

Architecturally the house is not memorable. Built in the 1680s, it was sold to a London lawyer, John Meller, in 1715. Meller furnished the house with impeccable taste, filling it with glamorous items of the day such as silvered furniture, the best silks, tapestries and china. No expense was spared.

In 1735 the house was left to Meller's nephew, Simon Yorke, and either a Simon or a Philip Yorke owned it thereafter. Philip Yorke I altered the brick façade of the house and consulted James Wyatt over internal changes and William Emes over garden alterations. He was, however, motivated by a strong antiquarian interest, and despite the severely unfashionable appearance of the house by the 1770s, he was more than happy to preserve every detail of his inheritance – down to the last seat cover. The successive Yorkes, who lived comparatively simply as rural gentry, were equally content to preserve the building. As a result, the elegant interiors John Meller created are more or less the same today. In the saloon are silvered chairs, covered in original Spitalfields velvet, gilt girandoles and very beautiful pier glasses of 1726, with grotesque heads and splayed feathers. The famous state bed with its Chinese embroidered hangings was bought in 1720 by Meller. The furniture made by royal cabinet-maker John Cobb was acquired in 1770 and, like all the furniture in the house, is in stunningly fresh condition.

The other unusual feature of Erddig is the eccentric habit the Yorkes adopted in the early 18th century of immortalizing all their servants in portraits and verse. A gallery of characters from carpenters to butlers is lovingly remembered in what is a touching insight into the workings of a house such as this. Having learnt a little about the people who ran the house and estate, it is possible to see exactly where they worked in the laundries, workshops, kitchen and butler's pantry.

2 miles (3 km) south of Wrexham, off
the A525 (map page 56)

FELBRIGG HALL NORFOLK

Felbrigg is characterized by its fine and varied 17th-century exteriors and equally interesting 18th-century interiors. It was begun in about 1620, and from this time dates the handsome, symmetrical Jacobean south range, built for Thomas Windham. Particularly noteworthy is the

The library at Erddig, a well-preserved example of 19th-century comfort

openwork lettering on the parapet spelling out GLORIA DEO IN EXCELSIS ('Glory to God in the Highest'). About 50 years later William Windham added the more sedate west wing (1675–86), designed by the gentleman amateur William Samwell, a little-known but accomplished architect.

The house was further modernized by William Windham II, who returned from the Grand Tour in 1741, full of ideas of architectural fashion and with a large collection of newly acquired paintings. The alterations were made by the architect James Paine. Out of the old staircase hall Paine created a dining room, the first of three very beautiful rooms. The following two, the drawing room and the cabinet, have exceptional plaster ceilings of the 1680s, although all the other detailing is later. The cabinet holds Windham's pictures, hung in the same arrangement as he devised; with its beautiful white and gilt chairs and scarlet wall hangings it represents a wonderfully complete 18th-century room. The pictures are mostly views of Roman antiquities sold as souvenirs to gentlemen on the Grand Tour.

Paine also added a delightful Chinese bedroom, with hand-painted Chinese paper and Chinese Chippendale furniture, and a Gothic library (1754–5) at the end of the Jacobean part of the house. With its spear-like finials on the bookcases, period globes and library furniture, it remains unaltered.

William Windham II was succeeded by the third William, who became a renowned politician – 'Weathercock William'. In 1863 'Mad Windham' was forced through bankruptcy to sell Felbrigg to John Ketton, a local merchant. The late Robert Wyndham Ketton-Cremer left the house to the National Trust in 1970.

2 miles (3 km) south-west of Cromer,
off the A148 (map page 55)

———————◆———————

FORDE ABBEY   DORSET

A long, irregular house of golden stone and crenellated parapets, Forde Abbey started as a medieval monastery and was adapted to use as a house in the 17th century. The Cistercians were offered the site in 1141 and the building was complete by 1150. Forde quickly gained a reputation for wealth and scholarship, and the architectural beauties of the abbey were augmented by the last abbot, Thomas Chard, who remodelled the building in the years before the Dissolution of the Monasteries. The quality of the abbot's work can be seen in the tower, with its double-tiered oriel window.

The estate passed through the hands of a number of families until in 1649 (the year of Charles I's execution) it was purchased by Edmund Prideaux, Attorney-General to Oliver Cromwell. Over the following ten years the house was created out of the abbey ruins. Prideaux reduced the old hall, turned the monks' gallery into an Italianate saloon with decorative oval windows, and built a grand staircase to service the new state apartments.

The saloon is a very lavish room with a complex ceiling of painted armorial panels and plaster reliefs of the *Murder of Abel* and the *Sacrifice of Isaac* in an exuberant, naïve style. Five early 18th-century Mortlake tapestries showing the *Acts of the Apostles* were made for this room, and were probably the gift of Queen Anne to Sir Francis Gwyn, her Secretary at War, who inherited Forde by marriage in 1702.

The monks' dormitory, with its plain vaulted ceiling, retains its monastic simplicity. This, like Thomas Chard's traceried cloisters and the 12th-century chapel, endows Forde with a romantic charm, and the chiming of the 15th-century clock bell, which once called the monks to prayer, seems almost to be testifying to the antiquity of the house.

4 miles (6.5 km) south-east of Chard,
off the B3167 (map pages 54–5)

———————◆———————

HADDON HALL   DERBYSHIRE

A charming medieval building, topped with battlements, Haddon Hall stands on a limestone hill overlooking the River Wye. Its history is one of neglect followed by careful restoration. The Manners family have owned the house since 1567, but after they became the Earls of Rutland in

Haddon Hall – the archway leads to the great hall

1641, they abandoned Haddon for BELVOIR CASTLE (Leicestershire). Haddon slipped gently into an undisturbed sleep, remaining quite unaltered until its romantic medieval beauty sparked the imagination of a descendant of the family, the 9th Duke of Rutland, who expertly restored the house earlier this century.

The building looks rambling and romantic; ranges of buildings from various periods huddle around the central hall and chapel in the usual haphazard medieval way. The hall with its minstrel gallery was built by a crusading knight who owned Haddon before the Manners family. The screens passage features a curious iron fetter, which was used to punish unenthusiastic drinkers at banquets. One of the offender's hands was held in the fetter while the spurned drink was poured down the sleeve. The kitchen is an exceptional survival, showing the full range of equipment available to the Tudor cook, from stone water troughs to the 'dole cupboard', a sort of breadbin on wheels. The chapel, which has Norman origins, has some beautiful 15th-century frescoes of St Christopher and St Nicholas.

The small museum in the lower court includes a display of lost possessions retrieved from behind the panelling and the floorboards during the 20th-century restoration. Rings, money, keys, even a shoe, powerfully evoke the sense of times past in this most atmospheric house.

2 miles (3 km) south-east of Bakewell,
on the A6 (map pages 55–6)

HAGLEY HALL WEST MIDLANDS

Hagley Hall was built from 1754 to 1760 for the 1st Lord Lyttleton, whose ten years as Lord Commissioner of the Treasury had greatly augmented his already considerable fortune. The Hall replaced an Elizabethan mansion. After considering many different styles for his new house, Lyttleton settled on a Palladian design by the gentleman architect Sanderson Miller, who a few years earlier had designed a large garden folly in the form of a ruined castle at Hagley. Externally the house is large and block-like, with a central pediment and four corner towers.

It was the Grand Tour which provoked, as it had for so many other aristocrats, the architectural interests of Lord Lyttleton. His interest in Italian art and craftsmanship, and the collection of *objets d'art* with which he returned from his travels, shaped the way the new house was decorated. Italian craftsmen were brought to Hagley to construct the flamboyant chimneys and ceilings, and the rooms were designed around the copies of classical sculptures and other treasures brought from Rome, supplemented by specially commissioned works by the sculptor Rysbrack. The White Hall – an enormous and sumptuously decorated room with plasterwork by Francesco Vassalli – held the housewarming celebration of 1760, an event which lasted three whole days.

The tapestry room, with its rich rococo pier glasses and console tables, contains tapestries woven at the Soho factory in 1720. In the Van Dyck room, its walls covered with vines and cornucopias, are several works by the great Flemish painter, including a portrait of the 2nd Earl Carlisle and the poignant *Descent from the Cross*. Also in this room is a striking picture by the 16th-century Netherlandish artist Marinus van Reymerswaele, *The Misers*, which shows two exceptionally wizened characters counting money. The

Continued on page 99

Guided Tour

◆

HARDWICK HALL
DERBYSHIRE

Hardwick Hall, arguably the greatest of Elizabethan houses, is a physical testament to the success, power and character of its builder, the charismatic Bess of Hardwick. She rose from the ranks of the lower gentry through a number of marriages to a position of extraordinary wealth and influence. Married in 1567 to the 6th Earl of Shrewsbury, Bess had bought the family home, Hardwick, from her impoverished brother a year earlier and, owing to a heated dispute with her husband over the ownership of their other home, CHATSWORTH (Derbyshire), she decided to put all her energies into her new acquisition.

Bess's first attempt to realize her building ambitions at Hardwick resulted in the Old Hall, now a ruin, which sits no more than a few yards from the house proper. Dissatisfied with this first mansion, after her husband's death in 1590, she and her master mason, Robert Smythson, created the New Hall.

Hardwick Hall rises in a compact rectilinear mass featuring six towers, each ornamented with a coronet and Bess's initials 'ES' (Elizabeth Shrewsbury). The vast area taken up by windows is immediately striking, giving rise to the local adage: 'Hardwick Hall, more glass than wall'. In her extravagant use of expensive glass Bess was making a clear statement about her modernity as well as her wealth, and the layout of the house is similarly innovatory. Contrary to medieval tradition, which centred the house on a great hall running parallel to the body of the house, Hardwick's hall runs at right angles to the façade.

The hall, like all the rooms at Hardwick, is lofty and light. The screen of columns, remarkable in its classical purity, was carved in 1597 by William Griffin. The plasterwork overmantel above the chimneypiece displays the Hardwick arms topped by a coronet and supported by two stags. Wild roses, or eglantines, were the family crest and appear here and all over the house. The massive central table is made from two pieces of oak each 27 ft (8 m) long and dates from the mid 17th century. The screens at either end of the hall hold two important sets of hangings originally made for CHATSWORTH out of a patchwork of velvet, silk and cloth of gold (some of which came from old medieval copes). The theme of the hangings is that of famous heroines and their virtues, a subject which undoubtedly held great appeal for Bess.

The state rooms at Hardwick are all on the upper floors, and are approached by

BESS'S INITIALS 'ES'

Right STRAPWORK

PLASTERWORK

and many of Bess's original portraits. The portrait of Bess seen at the High Great Chamber end of the gallery shows her austere in mourning black with a grand five-string pearl necklace. The canopy on the window side of the gallery is a piece of fantasy stage scenery added to the room for effect by the 6th Duke of Devonshire in the early 19th century.

The withdrawing chamber occupies the centre of the entrance front and is entered from the gallery. It contains several pieces of unusual furniture which Bess commissioned and which were listed in her inventory in 1601. Such high-quality furniture of this type and age is very rare today, and the superb walnut table supported by mythical beasts and the pedimented cabinet are justly famous.

Adjoining this room is the 'Best Bed-chamber', containing an early 18th-century bed brought into the house by the 6th Duke, and original tapestries of 1591. The Blue Room beyond, which has a bed dating from 1629, also has an impressive overmantel carved to depict the tale of the marriage of Tobias to Sarah from the Apocrypha of the Old Testament. This story of a woman widowed six times seems to have appealed to Bess, for she used it in several other places in tapestries and table carpets.

6 miles (9.5 km) north-west of Mansfield, off the A617
(map pages 55–6)

the broad main staircase. This long stone staircase, lit by windows at different levels, curves out of sight as the flights run up to the top of the house. The drawing room, on the first floor, is hung with tapestries bought by Bess in 1601. The early 17th-century Dutch marquetry display cabinet holds interesting pieces of blue and white china, including a 16th-century Ming jug. The staircase continues up to the second floor and leads to the most impressive room, indeed one of the finest rooms of its period in England – the vast High Great Chamber – 26 ft (8 m) high and filled with light from the huge leaded windows. The room is designed as a unit, the ornate plaster frieze, rich tapestries and chimneypiece all contributing to the magnificent effect. The theme of the frieze is *The Forest*; painted in naturalistic colours, it shows the court of Diana surrounded by scenes of country life. The tapestries, depicting the *Life of Ulysses*, were bought in 1587 and the room was designed for their display. The High Great Chamber was Bess's place for grand entertainment and dining, and although sparsely furnished when not in use, would have been filled with tables for special occasions. In addition to the suite of chairs (which are 19th-century copies of 17th-century originals) and the early 17th-century couch, there is the Eglantine Table, possibly made for Bess's marriage of 1567. The table is sturdy, with an inlaid surface of various woods showing musical instruments, sheet music, cards, chess and backgammon boards.

The long gallery runs the full length of the house. It retains the original tapestries

Continued from page 95

financial aspect of this picture is rather ironic considering that the 2nd Lord won it at cards.

The house was nearly destroyed by fire in 1925, and, although a great deal of damage was done, the building was restored by the 9th Lord Cobham to its original condition.

2 miles (3 km) south-east of
Stourbridge, off the A491
(map pages 54–5)

◆

HAM HOUSE   LONDON

Ham House was begun in 1610 for Sir Thomas Vavasour, altered in the 1630s by William Murray, 1st Earl of Dysart, and then enlarged in the 1670s by the Duke and Duchess of Lauderdale. They were an unattractive pair: the Duchess was known for her 'ravenous covetousness', and her husband, a very powerful politician, was described as 'the coldest friend and the most violent enemy that ever was known'.

Keen to reform their old-fashioned Jacobean house, and having created extra rooms by enlarging the south front, they began to furnish the house in the most lavish style imaginable – even the fire tongs are silver-mounted. Rich plaster ceilings, excellent woodwork, panelling, parquetry floors and fine lacquer furniture all testify to this uncontained extravagance.

Most of the furniture in the house was listed in inventories of 1679 and 1683 and its survival is remarkable. Notable pieces include a writing cabinet, decorated with oyster veneers (circular or oval veneers made by slicing across small branches) and ebony inlay, with silver mounts, and an ebony and silver table in the Green Closet. Many of the chairs retain their original upholstery, with complex fringing and rich fabrics. There is a ceiling by the painter Antonio Verrio, and several good contemporary portraits, including one by Lely of the Duke and Duchess in old age, which hangs in the gallery. They look down with self-

Left The formal gardens at the eastern end of Ham House

satisfied hauteur on their splendid creation which has stood largely unaltered for over three centuries. The house passed through the descendants of the Dysart family and was given to the National Trust in 1948.

On the south bank of the River
Thames, 1 mile (1.5 km) south of
Richmond (map page 55)

◆

HAREWOOD HOUSE   WEST YORKSHIRE

Glittering, elegant Harewood House was plain Gawthorpe House when Edwin Lascelles, 1st Baron Harewood (the title and the house are pronounced 'Harwood'), asked John Carr of York to build him a neo-classical mansion in 1759. The young Robert Adam, fresh from his Grand Tour, was subsequently asked to collaborate with Carr on the exterior, and later, in the 1760s, was entrusted with the complete decoration and design of the many grand rooms. Adam produced some of the most spectacular rooms of his career at Harewood, assisted by colleagues including Thomas Chippendale. Although the exterior was altered by Sir Charles Barry in the 1840s, the interior at Harewood survives as one of the most complete examples of 18th-century taste.

Nearly all the rooms at Harewood are significant in some way, but the entrance hall is worthy of particular attention. Painted in pinks, reds and whites, it has a striking harmony of composition and a decorative effect which is complete but not overdone. Similarly elegant is the gallery, with its Chippendale consoles and mirrors ornamented with cupids, garlands of flowers and painted panels by Angelica Kauffmann. The complex ceiling is painted by Biagio Rebecca, and a suite of gilt chairs completes the crisp, light ensemble. The swagged and fringed taffeta pelmets are very unusual – they are in fact carved in wood, painted and fringed to deceive the eye.

The music room has a ceiling of circular panels by Kauffmann, and the decorative theme is taken up in the specially designed carpet. Large classical scenes by Antonio Zucchi

Harewood House on its Victorian terraces, viewed from the south-east

(Kauffmann's husband) dominate the walls, while an elegant portrait by Reynolds, *Mrs Hale as Euphrosyne*, stands dramatically over the chimneypiece.

The quality of the Chippendale furniture is superb, notably the famous 'Minerva Commode' of 1773 which stands in the state dressing room.

Together with an extensive collection of family portraits, there are paintings by great masters such as Titian, Tintoretto, Veronese, Bellini and El Greco. The Sèvres porcelain in the China Room and the 17th- and 18th-century Chinese porcelain were collected by 1st Viscount Lascelles, the son of the 1st Earl, in the early 19th century.

7 miles (11 km) north of Leeds, off the
A61 (map page 56)

◆

HATFIELD HOUSE   HERTFORDSHIRE

The Old Palace of Hatfield, now in the gardens of the Jacobean mansion, was built in the 1480s for Cardinal Morton and later used by Henry VIII as a home for his two daughters, Mary and Elizabeth. It was here in 1558 that the young Princess Elizabeth received news of her succession to the throne.

In 1607, James I gave the Palace to Robert Cecil, son of Elizabeth's great adviser Lord Burghley, in return for another house, and Cecil, making the most of this exchange, went on to build a new, splendid and very large house next to the old building. An early death in 1612 prevented Cecil from seeing the house completed and the work was finished by his son.

The architect of the house was Robert Lyminge (who was also the designer of BLICKLING HALL, Norfolk), but Inigo Jones visited Hatfield in 1609 and was paid for drawings. Parts of the building, including the handsome central porch, with its three tiers of columns, have been attributed to him.

The great hall, already an anachronism by 1607 when the house was begun, is nonetheless a magnificent room which retains the traditional medieval layout of screens passage, minstrel gallery and dais. Elaborate wood and plasterwork and fine 17th-century tapestries set the tone for the rest of the house. In this room are two famous portraits of Elizabeth I in regal attire. The ceiling paintings are a Victorian addition.

The staircase, which had a great deal of the woodworker's skill lavished upon it, rises in broad, easy stages between joyful carvings of chuckling cherubs and roaring lions. The long gallery contains several royal relics, notably Elizabeth I's gloves and stockings and a crystal posset set (for drinking a kind of mulled ale) given to Queen Mary on her betrothal to Philip II of Spain. The north gallery has Charles I's cradle and a chair of state which belonged to Queen Anne.

After a fire in 1835, when many restorations were undertaken, the open loggia on the south front was glazed and

Hatfield House – a splendid red-brick Jacobean mansion

Hever Castle, the romantic setting for the courtship of Henry VIII and Anne Boleyn

renamed the armoury – an act which added, in effect, a new gallery of great novelty and beauty.

In the town of Hatfield, on the A1

(map page 55)

HEVER CASTLE KENT

Hever Castle is an exceptionally attractive moated forti-fied manor house. It was built in the late 13th century, then enlarged and altered by the Bullen family in about 1500. The thick external walls were perforated with Tudor windows, and the interior courtyard graced with charming half-timbered ranges. It was in this romantic spot that Henry VIII courted the fated Anne Bullen, or Boleyn as she liked to spell it, having tired of his first wife of 18 years – Catherine of Aragon – who was unable to conceive a male heir. This famous and fascinating love story, so central to English history, is re-created in the long gallery through the couple's haunting letters.

Hever had a succession of owners following the Bullens' fall from favour, and passed at first to Henry's fourth wife, Anne of Cleves, as a gift from the King after their divorce in 1539. From 1700 to 1900 Hever declined and decayed until in 1903 the American millionaire William Waldorf Astor bought the house and lavishly restored it – erecting a whole 'Tudor' village behind it as a service wing and extra guest accommodation. He also created sumptuous gardens, which lead, by way of wooded walks, to a large lake.

Although Astor's restoration was extremely sumptuous, it was also skilful and respected the spirit of the place. The exterior was left untouched and the interiors have been treated with consummate craftsmanship and panache. The rooms are rich with beautifully carved columns, panelling, doors and friezes, and not a discordant note is struck.

3 miles (5 km) south-east of

Edenbridge, off the B2026 (map page 55)

HOLKHAM HALL NORFOLK

Standing massively and rather forbiddingly in a 3000-acre (1200 ha) landscaped park, surrounded by the flat lands of north Norfolk, Holkham is the grandest example of a Palladian country house. It was begun in 1734 after its builder, Thomas Coke, 1st Earl of Leicester, had returned from the Grand Tour. In Italy he had become friends with William Kent and Lord Burlington, and he chose Kent as the architect of Holkham, which was conceived not just as a grand house, but as a showcase for the great numbers of paintings, sculptures, books and *objets d'art* he had acquired on his travels.

The house took more than 30 years to build, by which time Coke was dead. It was his great-nephew (also Earl of Leicester), the famous farming innovator known as 'Coke of Norfolk', who transformed the barren estate into a stretch of highly prosperous land.

The severity of the exterior of Holkham contrasts with the opulence inside. The splendidly rich Marble Hall, for example, with its Ionic columns of Derbyshire alabaster, was Coke's and Kent's attempt to reproduce the grandeur of ancient Rome. The state rooms on the first floor are hung with rich damasks and velvet and contain furniture and chimneypieces designed by Kent.

The art collection is superb, particularly rich in 17th- and 18th-century paintings, notably works by Poussin and Claude.

2 miles (3 km) west of Wells-next-the-

Sea, off the A149 (map page 55)

HOPETOUN HOUSE LOTHIAN

Nothing in the undramatic approach prepares the visitor for the Baroque splendour of Hopetoun's east front. The house was built for Charles Hope, 1st Earl of Hopetoun, by the architect Sir William Bruce in 1699, but in 1721 William Adam – father of Robert and James – was called in to enlarge and alter the building. The splendid entrance façade, with its rows of arched and heavily moulded windows, sweeping concave colonnaded wings and charming pavilions surmounted by cupolas, is his work and represents a pioneering achievement in the Scottish Baroque style.

The wings and rooms on the east front were decorated in a grand rococo style by Robert and James Adam after their father's death, but much of Sir William Bruce's work is intact elsewhere in the house, notably in the first Earl's bedchamber, which has interesting wall paintings executed by James Norrie. The state bed, which is a masterpiece of rococo design by Matthias Lock, was moved to this room when the original chamber was turned to use as a state dining room in 1820. The walls of the Red Drawing Room are hung with scarlet damask, and the elaborate carved and gilt pier glasses were supplied by James Cullen in 1766.

The staircase has been painted with a series of murals and *trompe-l'œil* scenes by the Scottish painter William McLaren, and in the cupola were recently discovered some extremely fine early ceiling paintings, which are thought to be unique in Scotland.

2 miles (3 km) west of the Forth Road
Bridge, off the A904 (map page 57)

◆

HOUGHTON HALL NORFOLK

This grand classical house with its four stout towers was built by Britain's first Prime Minister, Sir Robert Walpole, in 1721–35. Walpole chose the two most fashionable artists of the time to design his house, in order to support his status as the country's leading politician. Colen Campbell, pioneer of the Palladian style in Britain, designed the building, and William Kent decorated the interior.

Houghton is a showpiece of Kent's work, illustrating his versatility as well as his skill. He began his career as a painter, and the murals on the great staircase are examples of his work. As a painter, however, he was no better than third-rate, but as a furniture designer he was one of the leading figures of his period. Beautiful chairs and sofas in the saloon, the painted table in the White Drawing Room, and pier

glasses and console tables elsewhere all characterize Kent's bold, architectural style.

The state bed is the *tour de force* of the collection. Standing in a room with an impressive painted ceiling featuring complex plasterwork and gilt enrichment, it is stunningly grand. The silver filigree lace on the original velvet curtains must have dazzled when new, and the huge scallop shell rising out of the pedimented bedhead is like a great Kentian signature. Everything in the house is of a superb quality, including the doors, made of the finest mahogany. Rysbrack, the famous sculptor, contributed chimneypieces and overmantels for the Marble Parlour and Stone Hall.

The large picture collection amassed by Walpole was sold in 1779 by his descendants to Catherine the Great of Russia. Today it forms part of the collection of the Hermitage Museum in Leningrad. The quality of the current collection, however, remains high, including works by Kneller, Batoni, Zoffany and Reynolds.

After Walpole's death the house fell upon hard times. The male line was extinguished on the death of the antiquarian Horace Walpole in 1797 and the estate passed through the female line to the 4th Earl and 1st Marquess Cholmondeley. It was only in 1913 that Houghton was rescued from neglect to be occupied and restored by the 5th Marquess.

13 miles (21 km) north-east of King's
Lynn, off the A148 (map page 55)

◆

ICKWORTH SUFFOLK

Ickworth is an extraordinary house, and is largely the product of an extraordinary man – Frederick Augustus Hervey, Bishop of Derry and 4th Earl of Bristol (1730–1803). He travelled widely in Europe collecting works of art and filled his Irish houses Downhill and Ballyscullion with the spoils. Ickworth, begun in 1795, was his final venture in opulent exhibitionism and its huge scale was the result of his ever-increasing wealth, which came partly from his inheritance and partly from his bishopric. Sadly for the Earl-Bishop, he died of gout before its completion, while

The south elevation of Ickworth, begun in 1795

the works of art he had accumulated in Italy had been confiscated by the invading French five years earlier.

The building is dominated by a huge oval domed structure at the centre, which was to be the Earl-Bishop's house, while the long side wings connected to it were designed as picture and sculpture galleries. The original design was by the Italian architect Mario Asprucci and was carried out by the Irish architect Francis Sandys. The house was completed by the Earl-Bishop's son from 1821 to 1829. He had considered demolishing the building, but instead tried to rationalize the arrangement of the house by making the east wing the domestic centre and leaving the grand rooms for entertaining and the art collection.

The result of this change of emphasis gives the vast state rooms an impressive but rather 'unlived-in' feeling. The 18th-century paintings and sculpture are of the highest quality. There are some particularly good paintings by Reynolds and Gainsborough, but the star exhibit is Flaxman's *The Fury of Athamas* – a large sculptural group showing the mad figure from Greek mythology flinging his son to his death. It was commissioned by the Earl-Bishop in 1790 and cost 600 guineas. It stands in the huge entrance hall, which somehow feels as though it should lead to a national museum rather than a house. The top-lit staircase which rises from the hall was remodelled by Sir Reginald Blomfield between 1907 and 1909.

3 miles (5 km) south-west of Bury St
Edmunds, off the A143 (map page 55)

IGHTHAM MOTE   KENT

Ightham Mote is one of the finest examples in the country of a small moated manor house. The name derives not from the moat, but from the fact that a moot (council) met here in medieval times. The first known owner was Sir Thomas Cawne in the late 14th century, but the house seems to have been begun in the early 14th century. Many alterations have been made over the centuries, but some of the earliest parts of the house are well preserved, notably the

Ightham Mote, dating from the early 14th century

hall. In the 15th century Ightham Mote belonged to the Hart family, and in about 1506 it was bought by Sir Richard Clement, who added a timber-framed chapel, which overhangs the moat, and a cloister beneath. The chapel is beautifully preserved, with a wealth of original woodwork, including pews and pulpit.

From 1598 to 1889 Ightham Mote was owned by the Selby family, who were responsible for some 18th-century Gothick sash windows and some fine Victorian woodwork in the interior, including oak panelling in the hall by Norman Shaw (1872). The Selby family also carried out restorations that have helped to ensure the survival of the house to this century. It has been restored again with great sympathy in recent years by Mr C. H. Robinson, the last private owner, who recently gave the house to the National Trust.

3 miles (5 km) south of Ightham, off the
A227 (map page 55)

INVERARAY CASTLE   STRATHCLYDE

Presiding over the little town of Inveraray on the shores of Loch Fyne, the castle is as romantic a house as it is possible to find. Home to the Clan Campbell since 1474, when the 1st Earl moved to Loch Fyne from Loch Awe, the castle has witnessed much of the drama of Scottish history over the past 500 years. In 1743 the 3rd Duke began to rebuild his castle in the most fashionable taste, pausing during the Jacobite rebellion of 1745. He made use of an old design by Vanbrugh, modified by his architect Roger Morris. The result was a pioneering example of the 18th-century Gothic style, completed and furnished in 1768. The interior was largely the work of Robert Mylne, who worked throughout the 20 years it took to complete the project, creating a delicate French neo-classical ensemble.

The wall paintings in the dining room were created by two French artists, Girard and Guingard, who had also worked at the Prince Regent's Carlton House in London. Elegant chairs in French style were supplied by John Linnell and there are a number of pieces by famous Edinburgh cabinet-makers. Everywhere the style is light and elegant, with much use of gilding – a true reflection of Louis XVI taste. The Tapestry Drawing Room is hung with Beauvais tapestries of pastoral scenes, completed in 1787.

There are many family portraits, including fine works by Gainsborough, Opie and Ramsay.

1 mile (1.5 km) north-east of the town
of Inveraray, on the A83 (map page 57)

◆

KEDLESTON HALL DERBYSHIRE

Kedleston Hall, the vast, imposing home of the Curzon family, was begun by Sir Nathaniel Curzon, 1st Baron Scarsdale, in 1759. The architect initially was Matthew Brettingham, who was replaced by James Paine, who was in turn almost immediately ousted by the newly fashionable Robert Adam. Adam altered the entrance front only slightly, but the south front is entirely his creation. The centrepiece is inspired by a Roman triumphal arch and is approached by a dramatic oval staircase.

The stately portico by Paine leads the visitor into one of the most magnificent interiors of the 18th century – Adam's Marble Hall, where 20 Corinthian columns of pink Nottingham alabaster support a high coved ceiling of delicate plaster arabesques, modelled by Joseph Rose, Junior. Adam's aim was to convey the spirit of a Roman *atrium* (inner court), and the beautiful plaster-cast statues in the niches and the painted grisaille scenes from Homer complete this evocation of the ancient world. The room is sparsely furnished. It has been described as superbly empty, the only intrusion being some low stools designed in the manner of Roman sarcophagi.

At the heart of the house is the saloon. Based on a Roman temple, it is a circular room with a coffered dome ceiling 62 ft (19 m) in height, with coffered niches having cast-iron stoves designed to resemble Roman altars. The saloon contains more statues and grisaille paintings.

The state drawing room is hung with fine Dutch and Italian paintings and is the most sumptuous of the many state rooms. It is here that the famous exquisitely-carved sofas by John Linnell stand. The arms are supported by golden, trumpeting merfolk, each standing on a fish tail.

4 miles (6.5 km) north-west of Derby,
between the A6 and A52 (map page 55)

◆

KENWOOD LONDON

Set on Hampstead Heath, Kenwood is all that remains of a major country estate. It was bought in 1754 by the 1st Lord Mansfield, for whom Robert Adam remodelled the early 18th-century house in 1764. Having built the imposing portico on the entrance front, and added the decorative pilasters on the garden front, Adam created two wings containing an orangery and a library. The library is a beautiful room and often claimed as one of Adam's greatest works. The curved ceiling has delicate plasterwork inset with paintings by Antonio Zucchi. Sturdy neo-classical sofas stand in mirrored alcoves, and the carpet borrows motifs from the ceiling frieze.

Kenwood was purchased in 1925 by Edward Cecil Guinness, 1st Earl of Iveagh, who at his death two years later bequeathed the house and his superb picture collection to the nation. It is now known as the Iveagh Bequest. The

Kenwood was remodelled by Adam in 1764

collection consists mainly of English paintings of the 18th and early 19th centuries and Dutch paintings of the 17th century. The English portraits are superb and include one of Gainsborough's most ravishing masterpieces, *Mary, Countess Howe*. Among the Dutch paintings is *The Guitar Player* by Vermeer, one of only four pictures by this rare and precious master in British public collections (the other three are in the National Galleries of London and Edinburgh). The painting that is really worth a pilgrimage, however, is a majestic self-portrait by Rembrandt.

On Hampstead Heath, off the B519
Hampstead Lane (map page 55)

◆

KINGSTON LACY   DORSET

Kingston Lacy was built between 1663 and 1665 for Sir Ralph Bankes, a Royalist whose fortunes improved after the Restoration of Charles II in 1660. The architect was Sir Roger Pratt, who was a scholarly amateur, but a highly influential designer. The type of house he built here – in red brick with a hipped roof and dormer windows – was imitated in countless Restoration houses. Only the basic shape of Pratt's house can now be seen, however, for in 1835–46 it was substantially altered by Sir Charles Barry, who encased the brick building in Chilmark stone, added tall corner chimneys and an enlarged, ornamented attic storey, and created a new entrance by lowering the north side at basement level. Barry's Carrara marble staircase is one of his finest achievements, conveying the impression,

as intended, that the visitor has entered some grandiose Italian *palazzo*. His work was carried out for W. J. Bankes, a friend of Byron and a great lover of Italian culture.

The interest of the house lies as much in the Bankes family art collection as in the architecture. It is particularly rich in Italian pictures, the most remarkable work being a large, strange, unfinished *Judgement of Solomon* dating from about 1508. It used to be attributed to the mysterious Giorgione, one of the most romantic figures in the history of art, but it is now thought to be by his contemporary Sebastiano del Piombo. When it was displayed in the great exhibition of Venetian paintings at the Royal Academy in London in 1983–4, it was one of the most talked-about pictures in the show.

1 mile (1.5 km) west of Wimborne, on
the B3082 (map pages 54–5)

◆

KINGSTON LISLE   OXFORDSHIRE

Although built in 1677 with many of the features of an early Baroque house, Kingston Lisle is more famous for its exceptional Regency staircase hall, dating from the remodelling of about 1820. The architect responsible for this *tour de force* is not known, but whoever he was, he was certainly inspired. The staircase rises and criss-crosses in two graceful unsupported flights. The effect is very unusual and a kind of rural response to the exciting classical architecture of Sir John Soane and C. R. Cockerell (Cockerell, indeed, has been suggested as the architect).

The morning room, which has kept its original panelling dating from 1677, has excellent pieces of 18th-century furniture, some of which are in lacquer (an oriental form of painted decoration, consisting of coats of varnish made of shellac). There is an interesting collection of miniature furniture – pieces made by apprentices for practice or as samples; the details are astonishingly fine.

Needlework figures prominently in all the rooms, and the present owner's grandmother made the stools and firescreen in the drawing room, the coverings for the chairs and the needlework carpet. The octagonal carpet of the sitting room in *gros point* and *petit point*, designed with garlands of flowers, earns particular admiration – it took seven years to make. Among the interesting pictures is Marcus Gheeraerts' portrait of Lady Raleigh. Born Bess Throckmorton, she married Sir Walter against Elizabeth I's will and they were punished by a short imprisonment in the Tower of London. There is also an 18th-century view of London by Paul Sandby.

5 miles (8 km) west of Wantage, on the
B4507 (map page 55)

KNOLE KENT

One of the largest houses in England, Knole, it is said, has a room for every day of the year. It is a place of grand rooms and long shadowy corridors, its broad oak floorboards worn smooth with time, the ancient furniture awaiting a stately visitation. Standing in the house's tranquil courtyards, it is easy to conjure up the glories of Knole in its prime.

The house is largely the work of two men. Between 1456 and 1486 Archbishop Bourchier built most of what we see today. It then passed to the Crown at the Dissolution of the Monasteries and Elizabeth I gave it to her cousin Thomas Sackville in 1566. He added Dutch bell gables and Sackville crest finials outside and created a bold new interior within. The hall ceiling was lowered and plastered and an elaborately carved screen installed. The staircase is his work

and it is beautifully painted with vaguely classical motifs.

Knole is famous for its furniture collection as well as for its architecture. The 6th Earl of Dorset, Lord Chamberlain to William III, exercised his perquisite to take the furniture of the deceased monarch, and it was through this channel that most of the late 17th-century furniture came to Knole, complete with original fabrics and trimmings. Even the beds, most of which were at one time in royal possession, are complete to the last ostrich plume. The beauty and intricacy of the detail, colour and design is a constant delight. The silver furniture in the King's Room dates from Charles II's reign and is a very rare survival (such furniture was often melted down in times of financial crisis); recent research suggests that the suite was made by the King's cabinet-maker.

The excellent collection of paintings includes a room containing ten portraits by Reynolds and there are several works by Van Dyck. A nude sculpture of the mistress of the 3rd Duke of Dorset – the dancer Giannetta Baccelli – lies coyly at the foot of the great staircase.

In a park on the east side of Sevenoaks,
21 miles (34 km) south-east of London,
on the A21 (map page 55)

LACOCK ABBEY WILTSHIRE

Many country houses have retained the word 'abbey' in their name as a vestige of their monastic origins. Lacock is one of the few which also retains most of its monastic appearance, to form a hybrid – part house and part medieval convent.

Ela, Countess of Salisbury, founded the house at Lacock in 1232 and became the first abbess. Functioning as a convent until the Dissolution in 1539, the house was subsequently acquired by William Sharington. Sharington was one of a new class of Tudor profiteers and ran the Bristol Mint. Somewhat unscrupulous, he was attainted for debasing the coinage to benefit Protector Somerset's cause in 1549. It is to him that we owe the survival of the beautiful

The south front of Lacock Abbey, showing the oriel windows and tower by William Sharington

monastic elements of the house and also the addition of the unusual octagonal tower. At first-floor level the tower served as a strongroom, and has an octagonal table supported by four carved stone satyrs. In the niches in the walls Sharington kept his valuables and money. Sharington's niece married into the Talbot family, and the house remained in the family until 1944 when it was given to the National Trust.

The medieval cloisters and chapter house on the ground floor show how Sharington simply built his house on top of the existing structure. The vaulted ceilings and traceried windows are beautiful and remarkably well preserved, and in the Warming Room, where the nuns had access to their only fire, there is a huge steel cauldron made in 1500 and used in the abbey.

The entrance hall continues the Gothic theme, but in 18th-century rather than medieval form. It was built in 1755 by Sanderson Miller for John Ivory Talbot, and the ceiling is emblazoned with the arms of his friends in the county.

Lacock Abbey is noteworthy for being the home of William Henry Fox Talbot (1800–77), who inherited the house from his father and took up residence in 1827. He was a pioneer of photography, and his negative of the oriel window in the South Gallery, taken in 1835, is the oldest in existence. A museum dedicated to his life and work, containing many of his early photographs, completes a tour of the house.

In the village of Lacock, 3 miles (5 km)
south of Chippenham, off the A350
(map pages 54–5)

◆

LANHYDROCK CORNWALL

Lanhydrock is the epitome of the robust and romantic Cornish house. Approached through an avenue of beeches and sycamores, the 'E'-shaped building with its mullioned windows looks out over a formal garden enclosed by a wall topped with obelisks. The entrance is guarded by an ornamental gatehouse, a very picturesque piece of mid 17th-century design.

Sir Richard Robartes, a merchant from Truro, was the original builder. He bought the estate in 1620 but died leaving the house to be completed by his son in 1640. A terrible fire in 1881 destroyed most of the house apart from the north wing. This section houses the long gallery, which is 116 ft (35 m) long and rich with 17th-century atmosphere. The 24 plasterwork panels of the gently curved ceiling show incidents from the Old Testament in a naïve and delightfully jocular way. The interest of the remaining part of the house is in its gracious rebuilding as a Victorian country home by Richard Coad of Truro. There are good pieces of 17th- and 18th-century furniture and some fine portraits, including the romantic picture of the 1st Baron Robartes in his Stuart court dress of ribbons and rosettes.

The homely character of the house is particularly apparent in the kitchens, which are fully stocked with copper pans, jelly moulds, sugar loaves and all the other accoutrements of a working Victorian kitchen. A beautiful garden of rhododendrons and magnolias completes the setting.

2 miles (3 km) south-east of Bodmin,
on the B3268 (map page 54)

◆

LEVENS HALL CUMBRIA

This solid grey house of intersecting gables is surrounded by an ancient garden, with quirky topiary trees arranged like sentries along pretty paths. The house is largely Elizabethan, but began much earlier as a *pele* or *peel* (a compact fortified house characteristic of the English–Scottish border). The Bellingham family acquired the house in about 1580 and it was they who installed the panelling and chimneypieces of the great hall and the two drawing rooms. A new front was added to the south in the late 17th century by Colonel James Graham, who bought the house in 1688. It was for him that the splendid gardens, containing the most famous display of topiary in England, were laid out. The designer was a Frenchman, Guillaume Beaumont, who began work in 1689.

The 16th-century plasterwork throughout the house is of the highest quality and the rooms are filled with many

Levens Hall, built originally as a pele *or* peel

interesting objects and furniture. The great hall has the arms of Elizabeth I displayed in the frieze, and a delicate depiction of the *Madonna and Child* by the Florentine painter Bicci di Lorenzo (*c.* 1430) hangs here. The main drawing room, with its stained glass and pendant plaster ceiling, dates from 1595, and has a portrait by Rubens of Anne of Hungary. There are also portraits by Hudson and Lely and impressive landscapes by Cotman and Constable.

The small drawing room has other choice paintings, including an attractive Sickert and several paintings by Narcisse-Virgile Diaz de la Peña, one of the leading painters of the Barbizon School, a group of 19th-century French artists who pioneered painting in the open air. There are miniatures on display and a 13th-century Limoges enamel crucifix. The library and staircase have several Dutch paintings. Much of the furniture dates from the 17th century and includes a fine Charles II side-table with double barley-sugar-twist legs and four William and Mary torchères in the drawing room. In the small drawing room is some excellent Dutch marquetry furniture. The bedrooms have some fascinating early patchwork quilts made from pieces of Indian chintz in a variety of patterns.

Near the village of Levens, 5 miles
(8 km) south of Kendal, on the A6
(map page 56)

◆

Little Moreton Hall   CHESHIRE

This charmingly picturesque house is deservedly the most famous example of a half-timbered Tudor building. Surrounded by a moat and a garden of pretty walks, the black and white house, which is carved with intricate geometric forms, has subsided and lurched over four centuries into a structure of rickety shapes and sloping lines. The house was begun in about 1450, and developed as an 'H'-shaped house around a great hall. Extensions were added in 1480 and 1559, and the south wing was built between 1570 and 1580 after John Moreton inherited in 1563, but this remarkable house has remained largely unchanged since then.

The Moretons had been powerful landowners since the 13th century, and they retained possession of the house until 1912, although from the early 18th century it was rented to a series of tenant farmers. In 1937 it was presented to the National Trust. It is largely empty of furniture, but the interesting woodwork and construction afford an excellent opportunity to appreciate the skill and dedication of the 16th-century craftsmen.

The great hall, which dates from 1450, has a handsome oak refectory table and a 'cubborde of boxes', both of which stood in the room in 1601 (as listed in the inventory of that year). The hall was altered in 1559, when William Moreton II modernized the house and – in keeping with the movement away from the use of halls as a centre for household life – inserted a floor across the roof space and added two bay windows with delightful leaded glazing. This floor was removed at the end of the 18th century to return the hall to its original form.

The parlour has original painted panelling of the late 16th century, depicting the biblical story of *Susanna and the Elders*. The sunny long gallery is 68 ft (21 m) long and occupies the top floor of the south wing. Four sets of windows run along the sides towards gabled ends, decorated with plasterwork renderings of Destiny and Fortune. In the 16th century this room would have been used for exercise and games; an early 17th-century tennis ball was found behind the panelling here. The guests' parlour is complete with its original *garderobes* (lavatories) and an unusual

Little Moreton Hall, dating from the mid 15th century

'Secret Room', which is entered by means of a concealed door in the panelling.

4 miles (6.5 km) south-west of
Congleton, off the A34
(map pages 55–6)

LONGLEAT WILTSHIRE

Longleat sits grandly in the midst of a finely landscaped park. The self-confidence of its long, many-windowed façades is a reflection of the character of its builder, the brash, bluff, self-made Sir John Thynne, who bought the estate of Longleat in 1541 and began erecting one of the grandest houses of the period. The early building history of the house has proved impossible to untangle fully, but several stages were involved and a fire in 1567 may have destroyed much of what had been built before then. In 1568 Robert Smythson (later architect of HARDWICK HALL, Derbyshire) appeared on the scene and the biggest share of the design is often attributed to him. Certainly, the symmetry and lucid grandeur of the design, with the classical details handled with a confidence and subtlety new in England, suggests that an exceptional architect was at work rather than the more usual combination of patrons and master masons.

Successive generations of Lords Weymouth (a title granted to the Thynnes by Charles II) have transformed the interior in a variety of different period styles. The hall with its huge chimneypiece and heavy hammer-beam roof is probably the only piece of the early interior to have survived. Elsewhere, the work of the 4th Marquess of Bath (this title was bestowed on the Thynnes in the 18th century) is more evident. In 1860 he returned from the Grand Tour with a team of Italian craftsmen and promptly 'Italianized' the state rooms. The saloon, which was converted from the long gallery of the Tudor house, has two dramatic chimneypieces copied from the Palazzo Ducale in Venice. The extremely grand main staircase, flanked with portraits, was added by Sir Jeffry Wyatville in 1800, and at its foot is the family state coach, built in 1750.

Longleat houses many other treasures, notably paintings, furniture and books. Among the pictures are two fine paintings of the house dating from 1675 and 1676 by Jan Siberechts, a Flemish painter who settled in England and became the first artist to specialize in this kind of work. There are some interesting 19th- and 20th-century portraits as well as the more usual 17th- and 18th-century fare. The furniture includes the table used by the French diplomat Talleyrand at the Congress of Vienna (1814–15), which met to settle the affairs of Europe after the defeat of Napoleon. The library is superb and some of its treasures are usually on display.

Longleat was one of the first great country houses to be open to the public and it was one of the first to develop the idea that such a house could form the nucleus of a pleasure park providing entertainment for all the family as well as cultural enrichment. To this end, the 6th Marquess of Bath established a wild animal reserve in the grounds in 1966 and the 'lions of Longleat' are now as famous as the building. Subsequent attractions include a popular Dr Who exhibition.

In a large park, 4 miles (6.5 km) west of
Warminster, off the A362
(map pages 54–5)

LOSELEY HOUSE SURREY

Built for Sir William More from the stones of Waverley Abbey from 1561 to 1569, Loseley House is one of the great Elizabethan houses of the South-east. It is a transitional house architecturally, for although the main front is symmetrical, the centrally-placed great hall, with its projecting bay window, testifies to the medieval layout inside. Visited frequently by Elizabeth I, the house displays many patriotic symbols, such as the finely carved library overmantel with Elizabeth's arms, dated 1570.

The great hall has painted panels, and these – in addition to the grotesque panels in the gallery – are said to have come from Henry VIII's hugely extravagant palace of Nonsuch in Surrey, which was demolished in the 17th century. The full-length portraits of James I and his wife Anne of Denmark were presented after a visit to the house.

The enormous Tudor fireplace in the drawing room is one of the most impressive of its date. The ornate ceiling and frieze here, with its pattern of cockatrices and moorhens, was gilded especially for James I's visit. Next to the fireplace are cushions worked by Elizabeth I herself. Among the paintings are portraits of Sir William More with a skull, St Thomas More, and Edward VI. The coronation chair used by George IV can also be seen.

In the 17th century, Sir William's grand-daughter, Ann More, eloped with the great poet John Donne. She bore him 12 children and inspired some of the greatest love poems in the English language.

Apart from its artistic and historical interest, Loseley is now famous for its herd of Jersey cows, from whose milk superb dairy products are made, including ice cream.

2 miles (3 km) north of Godalming, off
the A3100 (map page 55)

◆

LYME PARK CHESHIRE

Lyme Park was given to Sir Thomas Danyer in 1346 by Edward III, in gratitude for services at the Battle of Crécy in that year. Danyer's daughter married Sir Piers Legh and their descendants lived at Lyme until 1946, when the property was taken over by the National Trust. The Leghs were noted huntsmen and soldiers and reared a breed of mastiff, something of a family mascot, intended as a companion of the battlefield. One of the dogs accompanied Sir Piers Legh II at Agincourt in 1415, and another – called Boy – was the faithful companion of Charles I's nephew Prince Rupert and was killed at the Battle of Marston Moor in 1644. It is said that the dog in the right-hand corner of Velázquez' famous painting of the Spanish royal court, *Las Meninas* (a copy of which hangs at Lyme), is one of this handsome breed, which is now extinct.

Externally, the earliest part of the house is the Tudor frontispiece (decorative entrance) of about 1570, an amazingly off-beat provincial design. From 1725 to 1735 the house was remodelled by the Italian-born Palladian architect Giacomo Leoni, who encased it in a classical skin.

Inside the house, remains of the 16th-century building can be seen in the finely detailed and carved panelling of the long gallery and drawing room. The drawing room also has a Tudor ceiling, with spiral plaster pendants and an elaborate plaster frieze. Leoni added the entrance hall, staircase hall and saloon, the latter being decorated with limewood carvings of flowers and fruit representing the Four Seasons, Painting and Music. A rococo ceiling, six fine early Georgian walnut chairs and a George II giltwood chandelier complete the room. The Stag Parlour, with its Tudor overmantel showing a naïve depiction of the house and its deer park, has a pair of carved Chippendale dining chairs, the seats of which are upholstered with pieces of the cloak worn by Charles I to the scaffold.

2 miles (3 km) south-west of Disley,
off the A6 (map page 56)

◆

LYTES CARY SOMERSET

From the 13th century to the 18th century this ancient and picturesque house was the home of the Lyte family. A row of clipped yews leads up to the 16th-century porch

Clipped yews lead the way to Lytes Cary

with its charming oriel window. To the left of the porch is the great hall, built in the 15th century, and to the far left stands the 14th-century chapel. The highest roof is that of the right-hand range, which was added in the 18th century to convert the building into a farmhouse.

The great hall, with its original braced roof and ornately carved cornice, contains a fine refectory table with some mid 17th-century chairs, and beautiful delft blue-and-white *tulipières* (made to hold tulip bulbs during the craze for the flowers in the 17th century). There is also a 17th-century birdcage in the form of a small house. The 'Oriel Room', which is really no more than an extension to the hall, was designed as a more secluded place for the lord of the manor to eat. The Great Parlour, which has early 17th-century panelling, has survived a period of use as a store for farm implements. There is a William and Mary laburnum wood table on six 'S'-shaped supports (the precursor of the cabriole leg), a lacquer bureau and an early 18th-century 'chest on stand'. The Little Parlour displays a collection of drinking glasses and a mahogany drinking table (designed to stand in front of the fire, so that one could drink and warm one's feet at the same time). There is a particularly fine Queen Anne walnut bureau in this room, with a domed top and extendible candle-slides in front of the mirrors. The Great Chamber has a carved and ribbed plaster ceiling of 1533, and contains unusual William and Mary cabinets.

Nothing remains of the herb garden created by Henry Lyte, author of the popular *A Niewe Herball, or Historie of Plantes* (1578), which was written at Lytes Cary and dedicated to Elizabeth I. The present garden is the creation of Sir Walter Jenner, who restored the house from 1907 and gave it ultimately to the National Trust.

3 miles (5 km) north-east of
Ilchester, off the A303
(map pages 54–5)

◆

MILTON MANOR   OXFORDSHIRE

Milton Manor was built in 1662 for Thomas Calton, and is a pretty example of the Dutch style that influenced country houses in the 17th century. The simple brick façade, with its elongated pilasters and steeply hipped roof, has a feeling of restraint and understated elegance.

In 1764–72 Bryant Barrett, who was the lacemaker to George III, built two wings to either side of the central block. One of these contains a Gothick library. This delightful room, with its delicate plasterwork and pointed arched windows and bookcases, retains its original paintwork, the lacy detailing being picked out in white. The architect was the little-known but obviously highly accomplished Stephen Wright. The Barretts were friends of Horace Walpole, whose Gothick villa at Strawberry Hill was clearly their inspiration. The Barrett family appear in a *conversation piece* (a type of informal group portrait highly popular at this period) by Joseph Highmore over the library chimneypiece. Also on display are fine pieces of 18th-century porcelain, including Worcester, Spode, Derby and Rockingham wares.

The chapel, which contains a beautiful *Assumption* by Murillo, has Gothick pews and is in a similar – but plainer – style to the library, while the Chinese Bedroom has a very fine example of Chinese hand-painted wallpaper.

In the village of Milton, 4 miles
(6.5 km) south of Abingdon, off the A34
(map page 55)

◆

115

Guided Tour

◆

MELLERSTAIN BORDERS

Mellerstain, built for the Hon. George Baillie between 1725 and 1778, looks out over terraced gardens towards the distant Cheviot Hills. The original architect was William Adam, who built the two flanking wings of the house in his robust, early Palladian style. He intended completing the composition with a Dutch-influenced centrepiece, but this was never built. It was left to his son Robert to add the central block in his distinctive castellated style. This was a style peculiar to Adam, seen also at CULZEAN CASTLE (Strathclyde). Mellerstain is the most angular and symmetrical example of the style, and to call it Gothic would be a mistake, for only the crenellations and the dripstones over the windows show anything other than a strictly classical simplicity and order. The severity of Mellerstain's exterior is in sharp contrast to the splendid interior, which displays Adam's style at its most intimate and inventive.

Entering the house by the east (William Adam) wing, the visitor passes through the Stone Hall, with its hearth decorated with original blue-and-white Dutch delft tiles, along the east corridor to the Small Sitting Room. The ceiling is made up of Gothic patterns in a geometrical layout – a most unusual composition for Adam.

The room contains a fine Queen Anne bureau and a pair of 'bell-back' chairs dating from about 1725.

The next room – the library – is the finest at Mellerstain. Simple in conception and delightful in its colour scheme, it exudes an air of refined comfort. Above the carved and moulded bookcases are four panels in plaster relief showing *Priam Begging Achilles for the Body of Hector*, *The Nine Muses*, *The Sacrifice of Iphigenia* and *The Choice of Hercules*. Over each door is a circular recess containing a bust – that to the extreme right of the chimney-piece is of Lady Grizel Baillie, wife of the first owner, carved in 1746 when she was 81. The central panel in the ceiling shows Minerva. Among the pieces of furniture in this room is an unusual William and Mary high-backed library chair.

The music room was designed by Adam as the dining room, something which is alluded to in the imagery of the exquisite ceiling. Delicate garlands of grapes and vines surround a central relief showing the sacrifice of an ox. The colour scheme here, as in the library, is the original of 1773; also original is the Adam pier glass with its carved and gilded sphinxes. This room has a portrait by Ramsay of the Hon. George Baillie, builder of Mellerstain, and a portrait of his wife by Gainsborough. The drawing

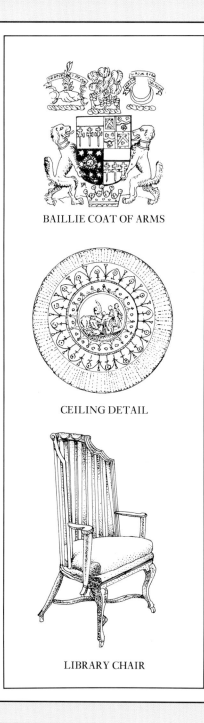

BAILLIE COAT OF ARMS

CEILING DETAIL

LIBRARY CHAIR

The terrace gardens on the south side of Mellerstain were laid out in 1909

room continues the Adam decoration and has a fine Napoleon III Aubusson carpet. The distinguished paintings in this room include a very beautiful portrait of Isabella d'Este from the circle of Parmigianino, two Ramsay portraits and a landscape by the Dutch master Jacob van Ruisdael.

At the end of the west corridor is the main staircase – a dramatic conception of two flights rising to a flying bridge and a gallery. There are four bedrooms open to the public, with original wallpapers and furnishings, and the bed in the Manchineel Bedroom has very attractive George III crewel-work hangings.

At the very top of the house is the impressive Great Gallery, which has ornate plasterwork. The room houses fascinating 18th- and 19th-century clothes which belonged to members of the family.

The last room to be seen in the house is the front hall. Here hangs another portrait of Lady Grizel Baillie (1665–1746), shown at the age of 60 and demonstrating all the strength of character she undoubtedly possessed. She was a poetess and something of a national heroine, for as a girl of 12 years of age she carried messages from her father to an imprisoned patriot, Sir Robert Baillie. In truly romantic fashion she fell in love with, and later married, Sir Robert's son.

6 miles (9.5 km) north-west of Kelso, off the A6089 (map page 56)

MOCCAS COURT
HEREFORD AND WORCESTER

The Cornewall family acquired Moccas Court in the mid 17th century, and the present house was built for Catherine Cornewall and her husband Sir George Amyand, who married her in 1771. In 1775 they employed Robert Adam to design the house, but – possibly through the need for economy – they engaged a local architect, Anthony Keck, to carry out the work. 'Capability' Brown and Humphry Repton were consulted on the layout of the parkland.

Externally, the house is a fairly simple red-brick affair, but the interiors are more adventurous. The hall, in which a portrait of Catherine Cornewall hangs, is approached by some steps and is dominated by a dramatic staircase, which is cantilevered up to a semicircular landing. The South Drawing Room has a frieze of musical instruments, repeated on the chimneypiece. This room was originally dedicated to music, the family's passion, and this is reflected in the early 19th-century portrait by the amateur artist Ariana Egerton of her two sisters, one of whom is playing a harp. The present owner is restoring and refurnishing the house, and he has found excellent pieces of 18th-century furniture for this room, including a particularly fine Chippendale commode.

The Circular Drawing Room, dating from 1781, is the outstanding room in the house. Adam designed the ceiling, frieze, doorcases and chimneypiece, and the room is an exceptionally pretty example of the late 18th-century taste for lavishly detailed and painted circular rooms, often used as boudoirs. The elaborate wall panels were printed by the Reveillon wallpaper factory in Paris.

11 miles (17.5 km) west of Hereford, off
the B4352 (map page 54)

◆

MONTACUTE HOUSE   SOMERSET

Built of Ham Hill stone, Montacute House is a golden-coloured Elizabethan mansion of remarkable character. It was built for Sir Edward Phelips (died 1614), Speaker

Montacute House, originally completed in 1601

of the House of Commons and Master of the Rolls. There was no architectural profession as such at that time, but Phelips employed a master mason called William Arnold, and it is to him that Montacute probably owes its appearance.

The original entrance front was that to the east, which now looks on to the garden. Montacute is 'H'-shaped in plan, and presents its multi-windowed façade to a walled garden, with twin flanking pavilions surmounted by ogee-shaped roofs. The house shows an early, only partially understood use of classical motifs, which were arriving from the Continent at the time. The skyline is ornamented with balustrading, elegantly curved gables, obelisks and amusing statues of Worthies in Roman garb. The chimneys rising from the roof are in the form of Doric columns.

From 1785 to 1787 the 5th Edward Phelips moved the entrance to the west front, constructing a porch using ornamental masonry from a nearby house. Although the new porch is slightly earlier in date, and features a mixture of Gothic and Renaissance ornament, it looks perfectly in keeping. The house lost all its contents through sales in 1651, 1834 and 1929. At the beginning of the century the Phelips family leased the house and Lord Curzon rented it from 1915 to 1925. In 1931 it was saved from dereliction and given to the National Trust, which has furnished it to an excellent standard.

Inside, the house has much decoration in strapwork (this was a popular type of ornament – introduced from the Low

Countries – consisting of interlaced bands and similar forms resembling elaborately cut strips of leather or parchment). In the screens passage is a piece of native humour: a large plasterwork relief showing the humiliation of a hen-pecked husband.

The gallery at the top of the house runs its whole length of 172 ft (52 m). Sparsely furnished, as it was in 1601, with authentic rush matting, this room is now hung with portraits of the 16th and 17th centuries on loan from the National Portrait Gallery in London, for which Montacute functions as an outstation.

In the village of Montacute, 4 miles
(6.5 km) west of Yeovil, on the A3088
(map pages 54–5)

NEWBY HALL   NORTH YORKSHIRE

Newby was begun in 1705 for Sir Edward Blackett, whose fortune came from coal-mining. In 1748 the house was sold to Richard Weddell, who gave it to his son William. William returned from the Grand Tour in 1765 with a fine collection of antique sculpture and determined to update the red-brick house and decorate it in the finest neo-classical manner of the day. He chose the best man for the job, the great Robert Adam, and Newby is one of the most splendid examples of the Adam/Chippendale partnership. In addition to redecorating the main rooms of the house, Adam added two wings – one to house the kitchens, the other to display Weddell's prized sculptures. More intimate in scale than the grandest Adam houses, Newby Hall shows exquisite delicacy and lightness of touch. Newby passed on Weddell's death in 1792 to his cousin Thomas Robinson, 3rd Earl Grantham, who made further alterations, including the addition of a Regency dining room. This now contains the superb Chippendale dining chairs, side-tables, sideboards and urns. Above this room is a billiard room of 1874. This was added in the Gothic Revival style of that time and is heavy with oak beams and mock-Tudor fireplaces.

The tapestry room at Newby was designed by Adam specifically for a set of Gobelin tapestries depicting the *Loves of the Gods*. The colours are well preserved and picked up in the original needlework on the chairs supplied by Chippendale. The exquisite door handles and lock escutcheons in this room, all designed by Adam, display his exceptional attention to detail.

The stucco relief plasterwork by Joseph Rose throughout the house is always refined, but particularly so in the entrance hall and in the Sculpture Gallery. The sculpture collection remains exactly as Adam and Weddell left it in its three-roomed gallery, lit from the top by a central dome. Here Adam felt he had achieved 'a meticulous reconstruction of a Roman interior'.

4 miles (6.5 km) south-east of Ripon, on
the B6265 (map page 56)

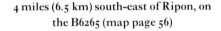

NEWSTEAD ABBEY   NOTTINGHAMSHIRE

Sir John Byron of Colwick bought Newstead Abbey from Henry VIII in 1539 after the Dissolution of the Monasteries. The price was £810. Out of the ecclesiastical ruins he fashioned a romantic house and started a line that by 1643 had been elevated to a barony. The Byrons had a reputation for wildness, eccentricity and extravagance, and these traits flourished most abundantly and most famously in the last of their line – the handsome and outrageous Romantic poet George Gordon, 6th Lord Byron.

The poet inherited Newstead from his great-uncle – the 'Wicked Lord' – when he was a boy of ten. It was a perfect home for a romantic such as he, with its Gothic ruins and ghostly air. Despite the decayed and mortgaged condition of the estate, Byron risked the wrath of his venomous mother by refurbishing the house on a lavish scale. The consequences were extreme – she died, it was reported, in a fit of rage upon opening an upholsterer's bill.

Although Byron loved Newstead, the pressures of his notoriety forced him into a kind of exile on the Continent and in 1818 he sold the family home to a rich financier,

Colonel Wildman, for almost £100,000 to pay off his debts. In 1931 the house was given to Nottingham City by Sir Julien Cahn.

The house contains many mementoes of Lord Byron's life, including portraits of himself and his friends, mistresses, wife and beloved dog – Boatswain. There is also a bust of Lady Caroline Lamb, whose unrequited passion for Byron turned to a hysterical obsession that scandalized London society. Manuscripts, letters and items of clothing complete this fascinating memorial to one of the most colourful figures in English literature.

11 miles (17.5 km) north of Nottingham,
off the A60 or A611 (map page 55)

◆

NOSTELL PRIORY   WEST YORKSHIRE

The remains of the 12th-century priory were bought by Rowland Winn in 1654, a few years before his brother was elevated to a baronetcy by Charles II. The 4th Baronet, Sir Rowland Winn, commissioned James Paine to build a large new classical mansion in 1733. Paine designed the entrance front we see today, with its broad, sturdy portico, and created elegant rococo interiors for the dining, Amber and breakfast rooms, the state bedchamber and the two grand staircases – one of which served the family, the other their guests.

After the succession of the 5th Baronet in 1765, Robert Adam was called upon to replace Paine and to complete and enlarge the house in the fashionable neo-classical style. He produced lavish schemes for the top hall, library, billiard and tapestry rooms, adding chimneypieces and ornate plaster decorations in some of the earlier rooms. The rooms were equipped with fine furniture supplied by Thomas Chippendale, many of them made to Adam's design. The state bedroom has a suite of green and gold lacquered furniture, famous for its chinoiserie extravagance. It stands against hand-painted Chinese paper which was supplied along with the furniture.

The beauty of the furnishings in these state rooms is echoed in the delightful doll's house, reputedly made by Chippendale as a young man while living at nearby Otley. Every detail of a mid-Georgian house is reproduced in fascinating accuracy, and the turned balustrade of the grand staircase is astonishingly delicate.

6 miles (9.5 km) south-east of
Wakefield, off the A638 (map page 56)

◆

OSTERLEY PARK   LONDON

Standing in its tranquil park, several miles from the heart of London, Osterley is an oasis of 18th-century beauty. Externally, the house is unusual. The body of the building is the Elizabethan house of Sir Thomas Gresham, founder of the London Royal Exchange, dating from about 1575. Between 1761 and 1780 Robert Adam transformed the square, red-brick house with its four corner towers into the model of neo-classical fashion we see today.

Adam's reworking of the old house was effected by the superbly bold stroke of slotting a gigantic open portico into the east front, creating a view into the courtyard beyond. The entrance hall is a fine composition of grey and white, forming a rectangle with an *apse* (semi-circular termination) at each end. The apses contain grisaille scenes by Giovanni Battista Cipriani, a Florentine-born artist who did much decorative work of this kind. The gallery, which runs the length of the west front, predates the Adam work in a

Osterley Park underwent a neo-classical transformation

heavier, more Palladian manner. The pier glasses and girandoles lining the west wall, however, are by Adam.

The tapestry room is decorated with Gobelin tapestries, designed by François Boucher, one of the greatest French rococo artists.

The most remarkable piece of furniture in the house is the Adam bed in the state bedchamber, an eight-poster designed to resemble the Temple of the Sun at Baalbek (a city in the Middle East famous for its Roman remains). Embroidered green velvet drapes hang from embroidered shaped pelmets, and above the fringing and tassels is the mighty dome, framed by sphinxes and swagged with silk flowers. Somewhat 'over the top', it earned criticism in its day from the waspish Horace Walpole who remarked: 'What would Vitruvius think of a dome decorated by a milliner?' The Etruscan Dressing Room finishes the state suite with painted walls in imitation of ancient Greek terracotta pottery decoration. A suite of painted chairs completes the effect. The house was given to the National Trust by the 9th Earl of Jersey in 1949.

In the borough of Hounslow, just
north of the A4, near Osterley
station (map page 55)

◆

PENCARROW   CORNWALL

The Molesworth family has lived at Pencarrow since the reign of Elizabeth I, but the present house is a square, elegantly simple Palladian building dating from the 1760s. It was begun by the 4th Sir John Molesworth and completed after his death by his son. In the 1840s the 8th Baronet, Sir William Molesworth, engaged George Wightwick, the leading architect of the region at that time, to alter the interior. He added a spectacular pedimented alcove to the music room to house a copy of a famous marble statue of Venus bought in Rome. Wightwick installed the maple-grained panelling from another house, Tetcott, in this room, and also in the entrance hall, which he transformed into a library. The music room's rococo ceiling depicts the Four Seasons. It contains a suite of Adam chairs, which were painted black when the room was used for the lying-in-state of deceased members of the family.

Pencarrow contains a good collection of paintings. In the library is a series of portraits of the Arscotts of Tetcott, who married into the Molesworth family in 1699. There are 11 Reynolds portraits in the dining room, as well as a conversation piece by Arthur Devis of the four Misses St Aubyn with St Michael's Mount in the background, painted in 1754. In the inner hall is a portrait of Charles I at his trial by Bower; another version is at ANTONY HOUSE (Cornwall).

The drawing room is decorated with rose damask taken from a Spanish ship captured off the Philippines by Admiral George Ourry in 1762. One of the treasures in this room is a beautiful 18th-century Chinese bowl, which depicts huntsmen galloping across the lawns of Pencarrow. It was probably painted in China from a drawing sent to the artist.

4 miles (6.5 km) north-west of Bodmin,
off the A389 (map page 54)

◆

PENSHURST PLACE   KENT

The Sidney family acquired Penshurst as a small fortified manor house in 1552. Subsequent additions, including some Gothic work in the 19th century, mean that, despite its medieval appearance, the house is really the product of five centuries of accumulated work. It was at Penshurst that Sir Philip Sidney – a poet and soldier renowned for his chivalrous conduct – was born, and his funeral helmet can be seen in the Baron's Hall.

The Baron's Hall, which dates from 1340, is famous as an unaltered example of a medieval hall with screens passage, gallery, dais and central hearth. The major beams of the chestnut roof are supported by life-sized figures apparently grimacing under the weight of their burden. Mid 15th-century trestle tables show the simplicity of one aspect of medieval eating, but the clamour, smoke and dirt of those days is left to the imagination.

The state dining room has a delightful Elizabethan

Petworth looks westwards across magnificent parkland, set out by 'Capability' Brown

portrait of Barbara, Lady Sidney (Countess of Leicester), and her six beautifully dressed children, painted by Marcus Gheeraerts in 1596. In Queen Elizabeth's Room is a late Stuart day-bed and chair suite, ornamented with carved shells and covered with a green and rose damask appliqué of 1695. A card table with *petit point* needlework in this room is attributed to William Kent, and the crystal chandeliers, which date from the late 17th century, are among the earliest known. The tapestry room, with its late 17th-century Brussels tapestries, has a Florentine cabinet with *pietre dure* panels (pictures made from inlaid pieces of coloured stone) and a Dutch cabinet which has a painted landscape framed in each drawer front.

The long gallery contains a number of gilt marble-topped side-tables, and an anonymous portrait of Elizabeth I hangs over a cast taken from her death mask. The Panelled Room has, in addition to the William III green velvet four-poster bed, some late 17th-century lacquer furniture. The Nether Gallery contains fine examples of sculpture and furniture from Italy and France.

In Penshurst village, 5 miles (8 km)
west of Tonbridge, on the B2176
(map page 55)

PETWORTH WEST SUSSEX

Petworth is set in one of 'Capability' Brown's most magnificent parks; the entrance lies at the heart of a pretty market town. The house is shielded from the streets by a high wall. The history of the estate can be traced back to Norman times, when it came into the possession of the Percy family, Earls of Northumberland. The present house was built when the Percys transferred the estate through marriage to the 6th Duke of Somerset in 1682. Work began in 1688 and was complete by 1696. The architectural showpiece of the house is the long majestic west front. The designer is unknown, but it is decidedly French in style, and it has been suggested that a French architect may well have been involved (perhaps the same one associated with

BOUGHTON HOUSE, Northamptonshire). A dome ornamented with classical sculpture once crowned the central feature, but this was lost in a fire of 1714 and never replaced.

Petworth is an exceptionally narrow house, being at most two rooms deep. The main front is composed of an *enfilade* of nine state rooms, with a variety of lesser family rooms behind. The services are confined to two separate blocks behind the house. An underground tunnel was created to connect them to the house, through which food, linen and coals were trundled in large trolleys.

The centre of the west front is taken up with the Marble Hall. This was the original entrance to the house and it is rich in architectural detail. The carving was the work of the 6th Duke's estate carver John Seldon, and the heraldic bulls and unicorns, which recline jovially on the door pediments, are splendidly naturalistic. The Grinling Gibbons Room contains one of the finest ensembles to be seen anywhere of this virtuoso woodcarver's art. Seven large portraits are framed with Gibbons' luxurious garlands and trophies, heavy with fruit, flowers, game, lace, musical instruments and jewellery. The detail is almost unbelievable, and at times the wood is pared wafer thin.

The nucleus of the art collection was assembled by the 2nd Earl of Egremont, who also had the grounds landscaped by 'Capability' Brown. His discernment was carried on by the 3rd Earl, who was unusual in collecting works by his contemporaries as well as Old Masters and in showing warm hospitality to artists. J. M. W. Turner, the greatest British artist of the period, often stayed at Petworth and even had a studio there. Several fine examples of his work hang on the walls. Other items worthy of note in the varied art collection include paintings by Reynolds and Van Dyck, some interesting antique statuary, and a mighty marble group of *St Michael and Satan* by sculptor John Flaxman.

In the town of Petworth, 13 miles
(21 km) north-east of Chichester, at the
junction of the A272, A283 and A285
(map page 55)

The entrance forecourt of Polesden Lacey in Surrey

POLESDEN LACEY SURREY

Polesden Lacey is an extremely attractive country house, whose simple early 19th-century exterior encloses an interior of sophisticated Edwardian taste. It was built as a Regency villa by Thomas Cubitt (an immensely successful architect and speculative builder) in 1821–3 on the site of an earlier house once owned by the playwright Richard Brinsley Sheridan. The client was Joseph Bonsor, a stationer. Polesden Lacey's yellow-washed walls are offset by louvred shutters and long elegant sash windows. The south front boasts an Ionic colonnade and above the entrance is a picturesque *cupola* (a decorative turret with a dome), which was added in 1906, at the time when the house was radically altered by Captain the Hon. Ronald Greville and his wife Margaret, a formidable society hostess. The notable art collection includes Dutch and English masters such as Cuyp, van Ruisdael, Reynolds, Raeburn and Lawrence, who is represented by the delightful *The Masters Pattison*.

The most fascinating aspect of Polesden Lacey is the insight it gives into the high society of the Edwardian era. The house, which was the backdrop to a glittering social circle that included Edward VII and the future George VI, ran like clockwork, with the aid of a small army of servants. Beverley Nichols commented of the period: 'Those were the days when women really did ensnare each other's chefs and kidnap each other's head gardeners.' Photographs, cuttings and menus all bring Mrs Greville and her times to life, making the house an absorbing journey into an era which has long since passed.

3 miles (5 km) north-west of Dorking,
off the A246 (map page 55)

—◆—

RAGLEY HALL WARWICKSHIRE

Ragley began as a castle in the 14th century, but the present house was built in 1679–83 for the 1st Earl of Conway. His architect was Robert Hooke, a friend of Wren and better known as one of the leading scientists of his day.

He was a competent but uninspired architect, and the glory of Ragley is seen inside, where James Gibbs completed the design of the house for the 2nd Lord Conway (1st Earl of Hertford) in the early 1750s.

Gibbs' masterpiece at Ragley is the great hall. It is a huge room – 70 ft by 40 ft by 40 ft (21 m by 12 m by 12 m) – decorated on walls and ceiling with some of the finest plasterwork of the period. The name of the brilliant craftsman who carried out this work is unrecorded, but it may well have been Giuseppe Artari, an Italian who was regarded as the head of his profession and worked elsewhere with Gibbs. The themes of the decoration are entirely nationalistic – a medallion of Britannia looks down from the ceiling, while figures of War and Peace face each other from above the chimneypieces. Gibbs produced further ceilings for the Blue Room, study and Green Drawing Room. The Mauve Drawing Room and Red Saloon were later modernized by James Wyatt in the 1780s.

There are very fine paintings at Ragley including portraits by Reynolds, Dahl, Kneller and Hoppner. The Small Drawing Room contains several equestrian portraits by John Wootton, whose charming studies (usually in profile) seem so much a part of robust Georgian taste. There is a glass and silver cruet set made by the master silversmith Paul Storr in 1804. The Red Saloon contains two important Netherlandish pictures – *The Raising of Lazarus* by Cornelis van Haarlem and *The Holy Family* by Cornelis Schut. Furniture of the highest quality can be seen throughout the house, but most important are the French commodes and Chinese Chippendale mirrors of the Red Saloon. The Green Drawing Room has a pair of candelabra by the celebrated metalworker Matthew Boulton.

The house was recently revitalized by the addition of a large mural by Graham Rust entitled *Temptation*, which fills the spacious staircase hall and proves that the grand manner of decoration can still be achieved today.

In a park 2 miles (3 km) south-west of
Alcester, off the A435 (map pages 54–5)

—◆—

The garden front of Rousham Park, viewed from the bowling green

ROUSHAM PARK OXFORDSHIRE

The house was built for Sir Robert Dormer in about 1635 and remodelled by William Kent for General James Dormer in 1738–40. Kent not only updated and refurbished the house, but also laid out a new garden, filled with classical temples and ruins, grottoes and cascades. The exterior of the building, however, retained its 17th-century appearance, and a reminder of the turbulent times in which the house originated can be seen in the holes in the oak entrance door: these were made by Sir Robert Dormer, a fervent supporter of Charles I, as loopholes for muskets in case of attack by the Roundheads during the Civil War.

Kent's first achievement at Rousham was the creation of the Painted Parlour. He painted the ceiling himself in imitation of classical *arabesques* and *grotesques* (decorative plant-like motifs), and it centres on a composition of *Venus and Bacchus*. The ornate carved overmantel standing over the Medusa's-head chimneypiece in this room is by John Marden. Within its carved frame is a painting of *Mountebanks* by the 17th-century Dutch artist Pieter van Laer. Kent also designed the sturdy marble-topped console tables and their matching chairs, and the many carved brackets which support the impressive collection of bronzes.

The Great Parlour was converted from Kent's library in 1764. The room has elaborate plasterwork by Thomas Roberts, and the pictures are encased in lavishly detailed frames. The chimneypiece in this room reflects Kent's interest in both the classical and the Gothic and combines elements from both styles.

In addition to the furniture and *objets d'art*, Rousham contains some fine portraits of the 17th and 18th centuries, notably by William Dobson, who was the chief painter to the Royalist side during the Civil War. The library contains a drawing by that genius of 18th-century caricature, Thomas Rowlandson.

Near the village of Steeple Aston,
12 miles (19 km) north of Oxford, off
the A423 (map page 55)

◆

St Michael's Mount perches precariously on a steep rock

ST MICHAEL'S MOUNT CORNWALL

The St Aubyn family have lived on this bluff rock, standing in the middle of its broad bay, for over 300 years. Approached at low tide by a causeway a quarter of a mile (0.5 km) long, and at high tide by boat, the Mount is surely one of the most romantic houses in Britain. It is easy to see why the rock was first colonized by Benedictine monks from Normandy, for whom it was an uncanny reminder of the great monastery at Mont St Michel. Between 1425 and 1660 the Mount played a more strategic role as a garrisoned fortress, occupied at one time by the rebel Perkin Warbeck, pretender to the throne of Henry VII. In 1657 the St Aubyn family made the rock their home, although the buildings there were not made truly comfortable until the 19th century.

The journey up from the small harbour of fishermen's cottages is steep but picturesque, with a splendid view across the bay. The house has many fine rooms centering on the Chevy Chase Room (once the monks' refectory), which takes its name from the bumptious and bucolic plaster frieze, depicting a hunt, created in 1641. The arms of Charles I are displayed loyally above. The two Blue Drawing Rooms, converted in about 1740 from the 15th-century Lady Chapel, are decorated with Gothick plasterwork and curved, pointed arches. The Georgian Gothick theme is taken up by the Chippendale pattern furniture and the ornamented

cornice. There are family portraits in these rooms by Hudson, Devis, Gainsborough and Opie.

The climax of the tour is the church itself. Built in the late 14th century after the destruction of the earlier 12th-century building by an earthquake, it has rough-hewn stone walls and pretty traceried windows. Outside, on the battlemented stone terrace, the view over Penzance and Marazion is one of the most beautiful in the country.

Island in Mount's Bay, opposite
Marazion, which is 3 miles (5 km) east
of Penzance, on the A394 (map page 54)

◆

SALTRAM DEVON

We have every reason to be grateful to Lady Catherine Parker, wife of John Parker of Saltram, for in 1743–50 she goaded him into transforming the modest Tudor house they had inherited into what is possibly the grandest house of the county. Her portrait by Thomas Hudson hangs in the entrance hall, and its inscription states simply 'a proud and wilful woman'. The Parkers' aggrandizement of Saltram reflected a substantial rise up the social scale – a country squire, John Parker II eventually became Lord Boringdon in 1788. The family developed a close association with the most famous artist of the day, Sir Joshua Reynolds, who was born at nearby Plympton, and the house is enriched by many examples of his work.

The morning room sums up everything which is most comfortable about grand Georgian living. Barely changed since Samuel Johnson saw it in 1762, this little room is lined with scarlet Genoese velvet and crammed with pictures. They are hung in a typically crowded Georgian manner, with small views interspersed with large portraits until only the smallest part of the velvet wall behind is visible. Over the fireplace hangs a delightful Reynolds portrait of John Parker II's son and daughter.

The spectacular Robert Adam saloon was part of the

Left *The remarkable saloon at Saltram*

fashionable alteration which John Parker II set about in 1768–9. It is a marvel of neo-classical ornament, rising through two storeys, with the design of the stucco ceiling reflected in the specially woven Axminster carpet. Adam designed the exquisite pier glasses, side-tables, sofas and chairs in this room, and they were supplied by Chippendale. As a counterpoint to the sumptuous grandeur of the saloon and dining room, the Chinese Chippendale bedroom and dressing room are delicate examples of the 18th-century taste for chinoiserie. The walls are hung with painted papers, while Chippendale supplied the exotic four-poster bed and amusing pagoda-topped chairs.

On the outskirts of Plymouth, 3 miles
(5 km) from the city centre, off the A38
(map page 54)

◆

SEZINCOTE GLOUCESTERSHIRE

The 18th- and early 19th-century fashion for things Chinese and Indian was usually restricted to furniture and decoration, but a few went so far as to create an entire building in an exotic style. The most famous example is the Prince Regent's lavish Royal Pavilion at Brighton, but equally delightful is Sezincote, the house which was the inspiration for the Prince Regent and his architect.

Sezincote was built by the East India Company nabob Sir Charles Cockerell in about 1805 and designed by his architect brother Samuel Pepys Cockerell (he was related to the family of the famous 17th-century diarist). It represented the first full-blooded work in the Anglo-Indian style, and followed Cockerell's more timid attempt at the style at nearby Daylesford, a house built for Warren Hastings, first Governor of India, in the late 1780s.

The house consists of a large, square block, built of Stanway stone and ornamented with pinnacles, minarets, broad scalloped windows and a wide overhanging eave or *chujja*. Surmounting the whole is a large onion dome. To the west of the house, an orangery stretches away in an arc and terminates in an Indian pavilion. The garden on this side has ornamental canals on either side of a fountain, in which the house is reflected – rather like a miniature version of the Taj Mahal.

The whimsy of the external architecture is not continued inside, where the interior is uniformly classical. A staircase rises in two flights and returns, via a bridge, in one. The bridge is supported by two decorative cast-iron girders, the first structural use of such a material in a country house.

The impressive saloon on the first floor is typical of the French neo-classical manner. It features a low, broad chimneypiece with a tall gilded mirror above, while the broad bay window is ornamented with sumptuous drapery. The fabric is caught up into swags, and held at the centre by a large eagle and at the sides by gilded lions. The saloon also contains two ivory chairs. The dining room beneath the saloon has been painted in the style of Thomas Daniell's 18th-century views of India.

The beautiful gardens are scattered with grottoes, temples, Indian sculpture and ornamental bridges. A stream runs through a number of different ponds before passing under the bridge that carries the road to the house. Beneath the bridge, suspended over the stream, is a stone throne where you can sit and watch the water cascading down towards a pool, from which rises a bronze statue of a serpent.

2 miles (3 km) south-west of Moreton-
in-Marsh, off the A44 (map page 55)

◆

SHERBORNE CASTLE DORSET

Sherborne Castle is exceptional in both appearance and history. Built by Sir Walter Raleigh in 1594 around a Tudor hunting lodge, it looks out across a valley to the old medieval castle from which it takes its name. It is a house dominated by towers, chimneys and lofty finials. Following Raleigh's execution by James I in 1616, Sherborne was given to the Digby family, who have lived there ever since.

John Digby, 1st Earl Bristol, enlarged Raleigh's house in about 1625 by adding more towers, making an 'H'-shaped plan. Although no other external changes have been made,

there are rooms decorated in the main styles of each of the ensuing centuries. The library, which has bookcases in the 18th-century Gothick style separated by circular niches holding busts, contains an exceptional collection of books, many of which date from the 16th century. The solarium – originally Raleigh's parlour – was remodelled in the 1860s as a dining room. The Red Drawing Room has several examples of the Digby ostrich, the family crest, in the supports of the 18th-century console tables and the coat of arms over the fireplace (it is also seen in the beautifully carved oval mirror in Lady Bristol's bedroom). The Red Drawing Room contains the famous painting *A Procession of Queen Elizabeth I* of about 1600, which shows her courtiers supporting the Queen in a litter. It is attributed to Robert Peake the Elder.

Other portraits here include works by Van Dyck, Gainsborough, Mytens and William Hoare of Bath. There is a pair of commodes by the Anglo-French cabinet-maker Langlois in the Green Drawing Room. The Oak Room, with its twin internal porches, was used to entertain William of Orange, who paused here on his way to his coronation in 1688. George III and Queen Charlotte also dined from the sturdy refectory table during a visit in 1789.

Near the town of Sherborne, 5 miles
(8 km) east of Yeovil, on the A30
(map pages 54–5)

◆

SHUGBOROUGH STAFFORDSHIRE

Shugborough was built in 1693 for the Anson family, who had owned the estate since 1624. Thomas Anson was a founder in 1732 of the Society of Dilettanti (a group of men of taste who cultivated the Grand Tour and antique art) and Member of Parliament for Lichfield. He extended the house with bow-fronted pavilions to either side of the 17th-century core, and also created a garden of temples, ornamental bridges and grottoes.

In 1774, Samuel Wyatt was called upon to add yet more features to the house for the 1st Viscount Anson. The long

Shugborough has undergone several additions and alterations

Ionic portico on the east front is his, as is the unusual three-storeyed projection which seems to cut through the centre of the building on the garden side. The extravagance of Viscount Anson's son, the 1st Earl of Lichfield, led to the sale of the contents of the house in 1842. Fortunately, the 2nd Earl was a great collector of French furniture and art, and it is largely due to him that today Shugborough is as beautifully furnished as it is.

Elegant plasterwork by Francesco Vassalli, dating from 1748, can be seen in the ceilings of the dining room and library. The dining room also has white and gilt side-tables with lion masks attributed to Matthias Lock. The library features classical busts and a colonnaded coffered arch. Wyatt's Great Drawing Room is an impressive room with a high vaulted ceiling and elaborate classical plasterwork. The gilt chairs in this room were made for it in 1794. The saloon is similarly grandiose in style, with its freestanding columns and a broad bay.

Among the pieces of French furniture collected by the 2nd Earl are works by some of the outstanding craftsmen of the time, including Jean-Henri Riesener, perhaps the most famous name in French furniture. The famous Chippendale chinoiserie display cabinet contains a dinner service given to Admiral Anson (brother of Thomas Anson) in Canton for helping to extinguish a dangerous fire. There is also a Wedgwood tureen from a dinner service supplied to Catherine the Great, decorated with views of English country houses. There are family portraits by many English masters. The grounds of the house are extensive and beautiful, and amidst the many garden buildings are some delightfully picturesque versions of some of the antiquities of Athens, including a diminutive Hadrian's Arch.

**In a park, 5 miles (8 km) east of
Stafford, off the A513 (map pages 54–5)**

◆

SLEDMERE HOUSE   HUMBERSIDE

Sledmere House was begun in 1751 after Richard Sykes, who came from a family of Leeds merchants, inherited the estate in 1748 and sought to replace the existing Tudor building. The third owner, Sir Christopher Sykes, completed the building in 1781–8 by adding two wings designed by the architect Samuel Wyatt, with graceful interiors decorated by the plasterer Joseph Rose. This fine neo-classical house tragically burned down in 1911, but not before most of the contents had been hurriedly removed – ornate doors were even lifted from their hinges. The building was restored during World War I by Walter Brierly of York to an exceptional standard, and today retains most of its 18th-century splendour. It is set in a fittingly grand park by 'Capability' Brown.

The house contains much excellent furniture and fine paintings, all rescued by the villagers in 1911. Notable in the collection is a double portrait of Sir Christopher Sykes and his wife by Romney, a Louis XV bureau by Dubois, and a suite of gilt furniture made for the drawing room by the cabinet-maker John Robbins in about 1790. The plaster-work is quite exceptional and is a tribute to the design skill of Rose and the restoration of Brierly.

The principal room of the house, running the length of the park front, is the majestic library, built to house Sir Christopher Sykes' superb collection of books. It has a Roman grandeur of conception, but also exquisite detail. The parquet floor re-creates the pattern of the carpet which was lost in the fire. The two white marble chimneypieces in this room were designed by Sir Christopher Sykes himself.

There is a blue-tiled Turkish room on the ground floor, the addition – after the fire – of the 6th Baronet, a soldier and diplomat who served in Palestine. It was designed by an Armenian artist to resemble a sultan's apartment. The room contains an important early 18th-century Canton enamel table.

In the village of Sledmere, 7 miles
(11 km) north-west of Great Driffield,
at the junction of the B1251, B1252 and
B1253 (map page 56)

SQUERRYES COURT   KENT

Built in what came to be known as the William and Mary style, this pretty house dates from 1681, some eight years before they came to the throne. With its central pediment, hipped roof and red-brick walls, it is modest and unpretentious, but a fine and complete example of the taste of the time. The gardens, which run down to a lake, form a pleasant setting for a house that has changed little across three centuries.

In 1731 it was bought by John Warde, whose descendants remain in possession of the house. The Wardes were close friends of General James Wolfe, who died in the victorious battle against the French at Quebec in 1759, and a cenotaph in the garden commemorates this hero of the early British Empire. Further mementoes appear in the house and powerfully evoke this period of British expansion and conquest.

Squerryes Court is little changed from 1681

The house contains a fine picture collection, including portraits by, or after, Michael Dahl and John Riley (who were among the leading portraitists in Britain in the late 17th century) and several works by Dutch masters, including the great landscape artist Aelbert Cuyp and Bartholomeus van der Helst, a contemporary and rival of Rembrandt. The drawing room has a painting of the Warde family on horseback (c. 1735) by John Wootton – a charming evocation of Georgian family life – as well as other portraits by Arthur Devis. A *St Sebastian* by Van Dyck is perhaps the most prestigious work in what is, for a house of its size, an interesting and wide-ranging collection. Other highlights include two mythological canvases by Luca Giordano and an equestrian portrait of John Warde by George Stubbs.

In the town of Westerham, 5 miles
(8 km) west of Sevenoaks, on the A25
(map page 55).

STANWAY MANOR   GLOUCESTERSHIRE

The first view of Stanway is from outside its high walls, in front of the imposing gatehouse. This rural example of classicism, with its shapely bell gables and mullioned

Right *The gateway at Stanway Manor*

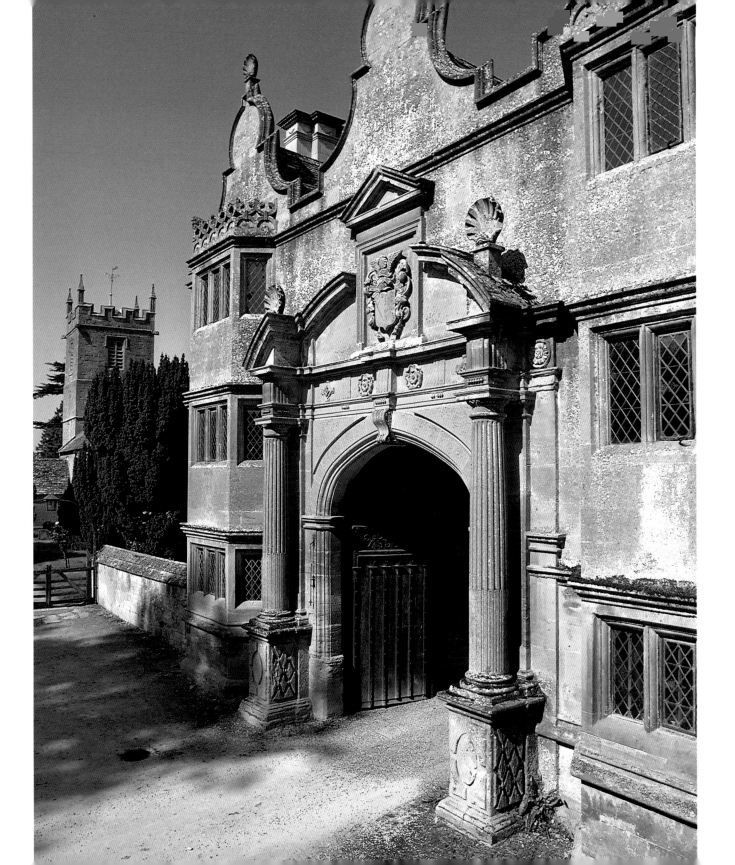

windows, was built in about 1620. The house it leads to was begun by Richard Tracey in the late 1550s, but was not finished until about 1640. The estate remained in Tracey ownership until it passed to the Earl of Wemyss and March in 1817.

The Earls of Wemyss concentrated their interests on their Scottish estates, and so Stanway remained unaltered and unmodernized. The house today has a timeless quality; the shovelboard (a variety of the popular pub game 'shove ha'penny'), which must have diverted many house guests in the past, remains in the great hall. This dramatic room is lit by the original glass of the tall bay window. In the drawing room are a pair of exceptional Chinese Chippendale day-beds. They were made for the Earl of Wemyss' seat at Amisfield House in Lothian in 1760, and with their delightful pagoda roofs add an unusual air of fantasy to this comfortable room. The Audit Room is a unique survival of a once-common country house practice – here, every quarter day, estate tenants assembled to pay their rent to the lord of the manor.

The remains of a water garden created between 1710 and 1748, and crowned by a stone pyramid in 1750, can be seen behind the house. Water cascaded down the steep mound into the lake beneath.

5 miles (8 km) south-west of Broadway,
off the A46 (map pages 54–5)

◆

STOKESAY CASTLE SHROPSHIRE

Stokesay Castle is not a castle, but a fortified manor house. It is probably the only early medieval house to have survived virtually unaltered and unmodernized to the present day. Sitting in the lap of a beautiful valley, the house is surrounded by a moat, now dry, and protected by a gatehouse and a curtain wall, with towers flanking a hall and solar range. Originally the courtyard was cluttered with small domestic ranges and outhouses, which were cleared away in the 19th century.

Stoke, meaning 'dairy farm', was granted to the Lacey

Stokesay Castle – in truth a fortified manor house

family after the time of the Norman Conquest, but in 1115 it was given to Theodoric de Say – hence the name of the house became 'Stokesay'. The North Tower was begun in around 1240, and in 1281 Stokesay was bought by Lawrence of Ludlow, a wealthy wool merchant, whose descendants owned the house for three centuries. Lawrence erected the present buildings surrounded by the curtain wall, which was much higher and crenellated at that time. By 1305 the North Tower with its projecting half-timbered top storey was finally complete, together with the domestic range and South Tower.

Although the buildings are unoccupied and unfurnished, Stokesay affords a unique opportunity to experience something of the simplicity of medieval life. The hall, where Lawrence of Ludlow's staff would have dined and slept, is lit by four tall lancet windows on each side. There were no louvres in the roof above the central hearth, so the big cruck beams which support the roof (and which originally extended half-way down the walls) are blackened with the smoke from countless fires.

The solar was reached by an external staircase. It was used as a sitting parlour and as a withdrawing chamber, and was a sign of gracious living in the early 14th century, for this was the only place where a modicum of privacy could be gained. It was equipped with decorative panelling in the early 17th century.

The gatehouse, which is an extremely pretty structure, was added in the early 17th century. It has beautifully carved corbels with representations of Adam and Eve, the serpent and the forbidden fruit.

In the village of Stokesay, 8 miles
(13 km) north-west of Ludlow, off the
A49 (map pages 54–5)

◆

STONOR PARK OXFORDSHIRE

Stonor Park has a long, simple Tudor façade of brick, which masks a house dating back to the 14th century. This façade, modernized by the introduction of sash windows in the 18th century, is terminated at one side by an ancient chapel. The chapel has played a dominant role in the history of the house, for the Stonors, who have lived at Stonor Park for about 800 years, are a Catholic family and for centuries suffered for this adherence to their faith. In 1581, at the height of Elizabeth I's measures against Catholics, the family was paying the modern equivalent of £50,000 a year in recusancy fines. The hiding of priests, particularly the Jesuit Edmund Campion, resulted in imprisonment, and because of their affiliations Stonors were banned from public office until the Catholic Emancipation Act of 1829. After this Thomas Stonor (1797–1881) entered Parliament and claimed the Barony of Camoys, which had long been in abeyance.

With the various struggles the family was forced to endure, the house and its contents were never given a great deal of attention. The Tudor house remained unchanged until 1757, when the entrance forecourt was remodelled, the great hall was gothicized in the fashionable Georgian manner, and a whimsical ogee-arched chimneypiece added. Between 1796 and 1800 the chapel was altered in a similar manner and a Gothick balustrade was added to the staircase.

There are family portraits by Romney, Kneller and Riley, and some interesting Italian works attributed to such masters as Tintoretto and Tiepolo. Among the fine furniture are some unusual pieces, such as the bronze and ormolu Louis XVI pineapple vases and a Regency shell bed supported by gilded mermaids and dolphins. A set of shell chairs, similar to the famous grotto chairs at WOBURN ABBEY (Bedfordshire), is also here.

Near the village of Stonor, 5 miles
(8 km) north of Henley-on-Thames, on
the B480 (map page 55)

◆

STOURHEAD WILTSHIRE

Stourhead has been the home of the Hoare family since 1718, when the banker Henry Hoare I (1677–1725) acquired and rebuilt the old manor of Stourton. He replaced it with a square house in the height of Palladian fashion, designed by Colen Campbell, the leading exponent and spokesman of the style. Henry Hoare II (1705–85) embellished the house's beautiful park, which lies around the lake formed by the River Stour, creating one of the principal landscape gardens of the day. Temples to Flora and Apollo, a Pantheon designed by Henry Flitcroft, and a grotto re-create the journey of Aeneas through the Underworld (as related in Virgil's Latin poem the *Aeneid*) in what is an 18th-century classical fantasy landscape.

In 1785 the estate passed to Richard Colt Hoare, and in 1791 he added two wings to the house, one containing his library, the other his pictures. Both rooms are superb examples of the taste of their time, and both were furnished by Thomas Chippendale the Younger between 1797 and 1820. Chippendale's furniture is remarkable, being both innovative in design and perfect in execution. The suite for the library, with its sphinx and philosophers' heads, is as sophisticatedly learned in style as his chairs for the picture gallery are light and elegant. Though little of his work – compared with that of his father – has survived, it is clear that he was a designer of genius.

The Hoares' varied art collection is especially rich in works by 17th- and 18th-century masters, particularly Italians. The *Marchese Pallavicini and the Artist* by Carlo Maratta is a splendid work by the artist who was the dominant figure in painting in Rome in the years around 1700. Anton Raffael Mengs' large picture of *Octavian and*

The entrance front of Stourhead, viewed from the south

Cleopatra was commissioned to balance the Maratta in the gallery. There is a bust of Charles I by Hubert Le Sueur, which came from the now-vanished Whitehall Palace and was sold after the King's execution. A similar bust of the King (several variants and copies exist) is at STRATFIELD SAYE (Hampshire). The beautiful *maquette* (preliminary model) of *Hercules* by Rysbrack was the basis for his life-size marble figure in the Pantheon by the lake. More fine sculpture can be seen in the chimneypiece in the saloon, which has ornamental plaques by John Flaxman.

In the village of Stourton, 3 miles
(5 km) north-west of Mere, off the
B3092 (map pages 54–5)

◆

SUDBURY HALL   DERBYSHIRE

Built over a period of about 20 years, from 1660 to 1680, Sudbury, with its hipped roof, dormer windows and cupola, is a fine example of Restoration architecture. The exuberance of the period is apparent in the elaborate interior decoration, as well as the sturdy Baroque double-pedimented entrance bay. However, the large mullioned windows, prettily patterned brickwork and old-fashioned long gallery all speak of a continuance of older traditions. The house was built for George Vernon, who in 1670 became Member of Parliament for Derbyshire, and it has been little altered since his day.

The interior of Sudbury is famous for its plasterwork and carving. Local craftsmen were responsible for the structure itself, but when it came to decoration of the interior, Vernon turned to the very best that London could offer. The balustrade of the Great Staircase, carved by Edward Pierce (a superb craftsman who did much work for Sir Christopher Wren), is one of the finest of its age in Britain and rises in a riot of huge curling acanthus leaves, with large baskets of fruit on the newel posts. James Pettifer was responsible for the ornate ceiling to which the muralist Louis Laguerre added a large painting in 1691.

The drawing room and saloon have carved ornament by Grinling Gibbons. The ceilings by Pettifer and Robert Bradbury have bands of floral motifs broken into geometrical patterns typical of the period. In the saloon are a series of full-length Vernon portraits, a giltwood George II chandelier and gilded lead wall brackets, which date from the early 18th century. A portrait of George Vernon by John Michael Wright, Lely's chief rival, hangs above the saloon door, and further portraits by this fine artist (less glossy but more thoughtful than Lely) hang in the long gallery.

In the village of Sudbury, 6 miles
(9.5 km) south-east of Uttoxeter, off the
A50 (map page 55)

◆

SYON HOUSE   LONDON

In 1762, when Sir Hugh Smithson, the future 1st Duke of Northumberland, called upon Robert Adam to modernize and aggrandize Syon, it was described as 'ruinous and inconvenient'. He left the exterior virtually untouched, and the square castellated house the visitor sees today is in essence the same Jacobean house that Henry Percy, 9th Earl of Northumberland, built in the early 17th century (it was, however, refaced in the 19th century). What Adam did, with his customary imagination and finesse, was to transform the interior into a setting fit for a prince.

The entrance hall and ante-room show Adam at his most stately and Roman. A double staircase rises gently past a bronze of the *Dying Gaul* (a copy of a famous antique statue) and leads to the ante-room, which is as colourful and extravagant as the entrance hall is cool and restrained. Twelve green marble columns (each recovered from the bed of the River Tiber in Rome) support sections of entablature which break forward to carry a gilded statue. The complex geometrical ceiling is reflected and complemented by the vibrant scagliola floor. The effect is rather like walking into a huge jewel box. Adam designed the plaster trophy panels which stand to either side of the door, as well as the side-tables which stand between them.

Continued on page 140

Guided Tour

In 1815, after the Battle of Waterloo, Arthur Wellesley, 1st Duke of Wellington, was hailed as 'the saviour of Europe', and it was only proper that the man who had defeated the mighty Napoleon should be given a house and estate appropriate to his status as a national hero. The circumstances of the creation of Stratfield Saye, therefore, were remarkably similar to those of BLENHEIM PALACE (Oxfordshire) in the early 18th century. Stratfield Saye is not a palace, however. It is a warm, atmospheric house full of mementoes, souvenirs and the possessions of the great man.

The house was built in about 1630 by Sir William Pitt and stood largely unchanged until refurbished by his descendant Baron Rivers between 1730 and 1790. Wellington considered several other grander houses before deciding on Stratfield, and when the estate was bought in 1817 he intended erecting a grand new house in the park. The painter Benjamin West produced a design for a new classical 'Waterloo Palace' of enormous proportions, but Parliament, perhaps mindful of the example of BLENHEIM, failed to vote through money for the project. The Duke, therefore, contented himself with the enlargement and modernization of the old house. The interior was totally refurbished to give every comfort for his old age – including the installation of central heating and water closets. The house has since undergone only minimal change,

Stratfield Saye, given to the 1st Duke of Wellington after Waterloo

A WYATT LAMP

BUST OF NAPOLEON

DRAWING ROOM DOOR

and affords a remarkable glimpse into the life of the great soldier and statesman.

The hall has pale blue walls and a balustraded gallery, and is decorated with banners surrendered by the French army on Wellington's entry into Paris. The columns supporting the gallery are an example of *scagliola* (plasterwork simulating marble). Inset into the flagged stone floor are mosaics from the nearby archaeological site of Silchester. On the sidetable to the right under the gallery stands a bust of Napoleon as First Consul.

The library, which has an early 18th-century ceiling, is thought to be the work of William Kent. The walls are hung with a recent reproduction of the original silk, and the room represents an authentic mid-Victorian sitting room. Over the chimney-piece is the *Ascension* by Tintoretto, and over the bookcases are portraits of Napoleon and George Washington, a lock of whose hair is in one of the showcases.

The music room contains mementoes of Copenhagen, the Duke's horse, named after the Battle of Copenhagen, and buried in the park. As the visitor moves from here through the staircase hall it is possible to see one of the Duke's original radiators still in service; the staircase banister dates from the original house of *c.* 1630. The Lady Charles Room contains paintings and furniture which belonged to Augusta Sophia Pierrepoint, wife of the Duke's second son. This room leads to the print room, decorated by Wellington with engraved scenes of landscapes and military subjects.

The gallery, too, is decorated with prints, but these were added in the 1790s, before the Duke's occupation, by George Pitt. The prints are separated by areas of gold leaf introduced by the 3rd Duke. The remarkable French Louis XV commodes by Etienne Levasseur are in *boullework* – a mixture of brass, ormolu and tortoiseshell (it is named after a great French cabinet-maker, André-Charles Boulle). A series of bronze busts on plinths represent Roman emperors and Napoleon in the guise of an emperor. There is also a bust of Charles I, a copy of one by Hubert Le Sueur.

The Small Drawing Room has a poignant portrait of the Duke in old age in the library at Stratfield, and the room is hung with the same original French wallpaper as the drawing room. The ornate plasterwork and the mirrors by Chippendale date from the 1750s. The fact that their rococo detailing is upstaged by the strongly patterned paper is true to the Victorian spirit of decorating. The excellent pictures were captured from the fleeing Joseph Bonaparte (Napoleon's brother, the puppet King of Spain) after the defeat of the French at the Battle of Vittoria, and offered to Wellington by the grateful King Ferdinand VII of Spain. The dining room, which dates from 1775, has a ceiling taken from the archaeological reconstructions of the ancient city of Palmyra. The Deccan Plate is a silver-gilt service presented to the Duke by the army in India after a successful campaign.

The Duke's life is commemorated in an exhibition in the stables. Many articles of his clothing are shown, including the first Wellington boots and the robes worn by the Duke at the coronation of George IV.

7 miles (11 km) north-east of Basingstoke, off the A33 (map page 55)

Syon House, built in the early 17th century

Continued from page 137

The Red Drawing Room has walls hung with original Spitalfields silk and a carpet woven to Adam's design by Thomas Moore in 1769. The coved ceiling is dotted with roundels painted by Giovanni Battista Cipriani. There are a number of important Stuart portraits in this room, including the famous double portrait of Charles I and his son, painted by Lely in 1647. The doorcases in this room are examples of the detail of Adam's work, and the sumptuous gilded mahogany doors are the height of 18th-century grandeur.

The long gallery is lined with delicate armchairs and decorated with elegant neo-classical motifs, which are repeated in the mirrored chimneypieces and side-tables. The Circular Closet at the end of the gallery is a beautiful little room; painted in pinks and blues like a Wedgwood vase, it shows Adam at his most whimsical, playful and imaginative.

**On the north bank of the River
Thames, opposite the Royal Botanic
Gardens at Kew (map page 55)**

◆

THE VYNE HAMPSHIRE

Reflected in the still waters of its large lake, The Vyne looks the essence of mellow tranquillity. The entrance façade, with its simple Georgian sash windows and imposing portico, belies the fact that this is largely a Tudor house.

The crenellated red-brick walls were built *c.* 1500–27 by William Sandys, one of Henry VIII's most loyal and trusted servants.

Having survived the political twists of Henry's reign and the subsequent upheaval of the mid-Tudor period, the family flourished. In 1650 John Webb, the 'nephew-in-law' and pupil of Inigo Jones, added the majestic portico to the main elevation, making it the first house in the country to have such a feature. In 1653 the 6th Lord Sandys sold The Vyne to Chaloner Chute, a renowned barrister, who ended his career as Speaker to the House of Commons under the short-lived government of Richard Cromwell. In the late 18th century, John Chute, a friend of the antiquarian Horace Walpole, added the rococo plaster ceilings in the Large and Further Drawing Rooms as well as the ante-room. After reworking the ante-chapel in a Gothick style, he added a 'Tomb Chamber' to the Tudor chapel, and it is here – in Thomas Carter's impressive monument (1775–81) – that Speaker Chaloner reclines in languid repose, dappled by the light from the 16th-century Flemish stained glass. Chute's principal work at The Vyne, however, is the staircase of 1770, which he apparently designed himself. It is the most imposing of its period in England and a masterpiece of wood carving and plasterwork.

Amid the excellent collection of furniture are four single chairs by the royal cabinet-makers Vile and Cobb and two marquetry inlaid commodes by Pierre Langlois. There is a Kent-style table in the vestibule, bearing the arms of Sir Robert Walpole, which may have come from HOUGHTON HALL (Norfolk). There are fine family portraits, Soho tapestries and 18th-century porcelain figures from Meissen and Bow. Above all, The Vyne has that comfortable, haphazard amalgamation of tastes and styles which comes from three centuries of loving occupation by one family, and it is this quality which creates its welcoming atmosphere.

**2 miles (3 km) north-east of the village
of Sherborne St John, on the A340 from
Basingstoke (map page 55)**

◆

WADDESDON MANOR BUCKINGHAMSHIRE

This huge French Renaissance-style palace looks as though it has been plucked by a giant hand from the banks of the Loire. It was built between 1874 and 1889 by a French architect, Hippolyte Destailleur, for the fabulously wealthy Baron Ferdinand de Rothschild (1839–98) to house his collection of 18th-century art treasures, and it is a show-case for paintings, porcelain, furniture and carpets. A building such as this has to be carried out with great panache if it is to succeed, and although there is more than a hint of vulgarity about it, this is outweighed by sheer zest. Many rooms are reconstructions of original French settings using old panelling and architectural features, although the furniture layout is definitely 19th-century in its informal style. Everything in the house is of the best quality. Thirteen of the beautiful carpets came from the Savonnerie factory in Paris, which made all the carpets for the French royal palaces, and the furniture boasts the names of masters such as Cressant, Carlin and Riesener.

Baron Rothschild's sister contributed a good deal of the china to the collection, including the exceptional turquoise Sèvres service of over 100 pieces. It was made for a Russian Admiral Marshal and is now kept in the dramatic blue-tented Sèvres Room. There are Meissen figures by the famous Johann Joachim Kändler (the greatest of all porcelain modellers) and exquisite Chinese wares.

The painting collection is particularly strong in works by 18th-century masters, both French painters (Watteau, Greuze, Fragonard and Boucher) and English (Reynolds, Gainsborough and Romney). Dutch and Flemish 17th-century masters are also well represented and Rubens and Cuyp figure prominently among these. In addition to the writing tables of both Louis XVI and his wife Marie-Antoinette, there is a secretaire standing nearly 14 ft (4 m) high, which is claimed to be the largest piece of French furniture in the country.

5 miles (8 km) north-west of Aylesbury,
on the A41 (map page 55)

WALLINGTON NORTHUMBERLAND

The simple, dignified façades of Wallington were begun in 1688 by Sir William Blackett, a successful Newcastle businessman, who demolished the Tudor building he acquired from the Fenwick family. His grandson, Sir Walter Calverley Blackett, modernized and reorganized the house in the mid 18th century and laid out the garden and the park (which includes work by 'Capability' Brown, who was born at nearby Kirkharle). Sir Walter was a man of taste and called upon the fashionable Francini brothers to decorate the dining room, saloon and library with flamboyant rococo plasterwork. On Sir Walter's death in 1771, the house passed to the Trevelyan family of Nettlecomb in Somerset. In 1846 Sir Walter Trevelyan inherited, and his cultured wife Pauline, Lady Trevelyan, made Wallington a meeting-place for artists and writers, particularly of the Pre-Raphaelite circle. Among them was the great art critic John Ruskin, who in 1855 persuaded Lady Trevelyan to convert the open central courtyard of the house into a covered gallery. It was decorated with murals on Northumbrian history by William Bell Scott, a Scottish artist who at this time was head of the Government School of Design in Newcastle-upon-Tyne. Among the murals the most remarkable is *Iron and Coal*, one of the first depictions in art of heavy industry. The stone columns were painted with flowers by Lady Trevelyan and Ruskin.

The Trevelyan family has produced two famous historians – Sir George Otto Trevelyan (1838–1928) and his son G. M. Trevelyan (1876–1962). There are mementoes of both (and of Sir George's uncle, the even more distinguished historian, Lord Macaulay) at Wallington. The house was given to the National Trust in 1941 by Sir Charles Trevelyan, brother of G. M. Trevelyan.

In addition to family portraits by Hoppner and Romney in the hall, there are works by Hudson and Gainsborough and a full-length portrait of Sir Walter Calverley Blackett by Reynolds in the saloon. Among many fine Victorian paintings can be seen works by Ruskin and Burne-Jones.

Wallington is famous for its porcelain collection, which came to the house as part of the dowry of Maria Wilson, wife of Sir John Trevelyan, in the early 19th century. The

hall contains finely detailed Bow figures and oriental porcelain. Lady Trevelyan's Parlour contains the finest European works of the collection, including a set of Meissen figures modelled by Kändler in about 1745. There is a small, very early Meissen teapot (*c.* 1715), and pieces from Sèvres, Vienna and elsewhere. There is also a Queensware Wedgwood service which was given to the Rev. George Trevelyan by Josiah Wedgwood himself.

The Needlework Room contains ten panels of exceptional needlework by Lady Julia Calverley dated 1717, together with a six-fold screen dated 1727. The other attractions of the house include a superb collection of dolls' houses and a particularly interesting 19th-century kitchen.

Near the village of Cambo, 20 miles
(32 km) north-west of Newcastle-upon-
Tyne, off the A696 and B6342
(map page 56)

WESTON PARK   SHROPSHIRE

Weston Park was designed by Elizabeth Mytton, wife of Sir Thomas Wilbraham, in 1671. Overcoming the prejudices of her age, she taught herself the principles of architecture, and taught herself diligently, as her annotated copy of Palladio's works readily shows. She rebuilt the medieval manor house in red brick with stone dressings in the fashionable style of the 1670s, to form a house of considerable grandeur. Inside, Elizabeth's rooms have been lost to 18th-century improvements, but the present owners are determined to retain some idea of how the 17th-century house functioned.

The entrance hall has a fine equestrian picture by Stubbs and the drawing room has portraits by Lely. The tapestry room contains Gobelin tapestries made for the room in the 1760s, and the suite of gilded chairs were made to match. The dining room has portraits by Lely and Van Dyck, while Holbein's portrait of Sir George Carew can be seen in the

Left The east front of Wallington

breakfast room. Jacopo Bassano's *Way to Golgotha* hangs in the West Marble Hall.

The house passed to the Bridgeman family, which was elevated to the baronetcy in 1660 and the earldom of Bradford in 1815. Sir Orlando Bridgeman was Keeper of the Great Seal to Charles II, and the sumptuously ornate bag in which this precious object was carried can be seen put to more humble use as a firescreen in the library.

The wife of the 3rd Earl, Selina, befriended the widower Benjamin Disraeli after the death of his wife until his own death in 1881. The 1100 letters he wrote to her are preserved here and are a fascinating insight into the mind of the great statesman.

Near the town of Shifnal, 7 miles
(11 km) south of Newport, at the
junction of the A464, A4169 and B4379
(map pages 54–5)

WEST WYCOMBE PARK   BUCKINGHAMSHIRE

Sir Francis Dashwood, 2nd Baronet, cut a dashing path through the high society of the early 18th century. Combining scholarship with a riotous drinking life, he helped to found two very different clubs – the Society of Dilettanti, which championed the cultural values of the Grand Tour, and the Hell-Fire Club, a drinking society notorious for its profane revelries, which met in a cave on the opposite side of the valley to the house.

Devoted to the enlargement and embellishment of his fine house and park, Sir Francis worked on the building from 1730 to his death in 1781. Although he asked advice from Robert Adam, Nicholas Revett and John Donowell, it seems that ultimately he acted as his own designer. The house is a curious composition. Visitors originally entered via the colonnaded south front, the double loggias of which add a distinctive Italian air to the house. The portico on the west front is today's entrance, and although it is grand and imposing, it seems peculiar to enter this long, narrow house on its shortest side.

Continued on page 146

Guided Tour

WILTON HOUSE WILTSHIRE

The land on which Wilton was built was taken from an ancient monastery at the Reformation and in 1544 given to Sir William Herbert, later created 1st Earl of Pembroke. Owing to a disastrous fire in 1647 only a small part remains of the Tudor house that he created, and the surviving section now stands curiously marooned between the rebuilding of the 1650s and the alterations of the 1800s. The great architectural showpiece of the house and the great problem to architectural historians is the stately south front. It was begun in 1636 for Philip, the 4th Earl, by Isaac de Caus, a French-born artist who was best known as a designer of gardens and fountains. A contemporary witness tells us that he had the 'advice and approbation of Mr Jones', that is, the great Inigo Jones. The front was damaged by the fire of 1647 and rebuilt by John Webb, Jones' pupil, and it is uncertain what respective parts the three men – de Caus, Jones and Webb – played in the structure we see today. Whoever deserves the greatest share of the credit, it is a masterpiece. Jones and Webb also collaborated to great effect on the interior of the house. Further alterations were made by James Wyatt in 1801–14.

On entering Wyatt's hall, the visitor is met by a life-sized statue of William Shakespeare by Peter Scheemakers. The first folio of Shakespeare's plays, published seven years after his death in 1623, was dedicated to the 3rd Earl of Pembroke and his brother, and Shakespeare's company performed at Wilton in 1603, during a period when the plague had forced the theatres in London to close. Two arches lead to the Upper Cloisters, which contain examples of 17th- and 18th-century sculpture. Numerous cases show mementoes such as miniatures and seals, Napoleon's dispatch box, a lock of Elizabeth I's hair and a pair of Fred Astaire's shoes. Among the paintings shown here are two views of Wilton by Richard Wilson and Jan Brueghel's *Winter Scene*.

The cloisters lead to the south front suite of state rooms, beginning with the Single Cube Room, so called because it is a perfect cube, with sides 30 ft (9 m) long. The painted and gilt panelling is ornamented with detailed carving of brackets, swags and laurel sprays. The richly painted ceiling (said to have been brought from Florence) is by Giuseppe Cesari (1568–1640) and depicts, amid scrolling arabesques, *Daedalus and Icarus*. Among the family portraits in the room are three Van Dycks and three Lelys. The furniture was designed by William Kent in the 1730s and added to by Thomas

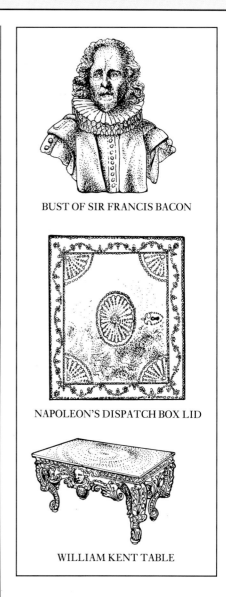

BUST OF SIR FRANCIS BACON

NAPOLEON'S DISPATCH BOX LID

WILLIAM KENT TABLE

Chippendale in the 1750s and 1770s.

The Single Cube Room leads to the Double Cube Room (likewise designed by Jones and Webb), one of the greatest 17th-century interiors in the country. It

The south front, built by de Caus under the direction of Inigo Jones in 1636–40

is exactly twice the length of the preceding room. As before, the walls are richly carved and hung with paintings. In fact the panelling was designed to take the family portraits by Van Dyck that make this room one of the greatest showpieces of his work. The most imposing is the enormous group portrait which dominates the west wall. It is 19 ft (6 m) long and 11 ft (3 m) high and shows the 4th Earl and his wife with their children and children-in-law. Their three children who died in infancy are depicted as cherubs. The ceiling paintings are by Thomas de Critz and they depict the story of Perseus. The furniture was supplied by William Kent in the 1730s; with its elaborate scrolls and masks, it matches the decoration in drama and scale. The mirrors between the windows were made by Chippendale in 1751–8.

The Colonnade Room terminates the grand suite and, with the Corner Room, it occupies the south-west angle of the building. The room is divided by a screen of 17th-century Ionic columns and the richly carved overmantel has a picture of the Madonna, surrounded by flowers, by the 17th-century Italian artist Sassoferrato. The delightful ceiling was painted by Andien de Clermont between 1735 and 1739. It shows the fad – very much an early 18th-century phenomenon – for showing monkeys up to various antics, often satirizing contemporary manners. The furniture, once again, is by Kent and there are family portraits by Beechey, Lawrence and Reynolds.

The Corner Room has a ceiling by Luca Giordano showing the *Conversion of St Paul*, and a number of very fine 17th- and 18th-century paintings, including landscapes by Claude and Rubens and a ruin scene by Panini. The Little Ante-Room leads to the double-flight staircase, added by Wyatt, and has a painting of *Democritus* by Jusepe de Ribera (one of the greatest 17th-century Spanish painters) and two terracotta busts of Sir Francis Bacon and Thomas, the 8th Earl, by Louis-François Roubiliac (a French-born sculptor who spent almost all of his working life in England and became the head of his profession). The staircase takes the visitor to the Lower Cloisters, in which are displayed a variety of dessert and dinner services of English, Continental and Chinese manufacture. The Large Smoking Room contains 55 paintings of the Spanish Riding School. They date from 1755 and were painted for Henry, the 10th Earl. In this room stands one of the greatest pieces of mid 18th-century cabinetwork, made by Thomas Chippendale and typifying the rococo style as it appeared in his pattern book, *The Gentleman & Cabinet-Maker's Director*. The delicately carved musical trophy in the central panel has a violin complete with strings. The Little Smoking Room has a rare set of walnut furniture dating from about 1670. The Gothic Hall, with Wyatt's Tudor-style Gothic vaulted ceiling, contains busts of Sidney, Lord Herbert of Lea, and Florence Nightingale, whose remarkable work in the Crimea was brought to public attention in the 1850s by Lord Herbert.

In the town of Wilton, 3 miles (5 km) west of Salisbury, on the A30 (map pages 54–5)

Continued from page 143

The rooms are very beautiful and many have painted ceilings by Giuseppe Borgnis in a style which is a hybrid of Baroque and neo-classical features. More geometrical neo-classical arrangements figure in the staircase hall and dining room, and these were painted by Borgnis' son. The tapestry room, which acts as an ante-chamber to the state bed-chamber, is hung with Flemish tapestries showing peasant scenes taken from works by David Teniers the Younger. The saloon and Red Drawing Room are exceedingly grand rooms and are ornamented with fine paintings, among which are works by Jacob van Ruisdael and Salvator Rosa. There is also some very important furniture, including two serpentine commodes by Pierre Langlois which stand among the best marquetry pieces of the 18th century.

The park is adorned with temples, grottoes and follies, including a Temple of Music and Temple of Apollo.

In the village of West Wycombe, 2 miles (3 km) north-west of High Wycombe, on the A40 (map page 55)

WIMPOLE HALL CAMBRIDGESHIRE

Wimpole Hall is an example of how a country house can form a cohesive whole even when it is the product of many generations and tastes. The central block of this long, red-brick building is the 17th-century house of Sir Thomas Chicheley, a member of the Royal Society, who built a small house, perhaps of his own design, in 1641. In 1686 the estate was sold to Charles Robartes, 2nd Earl of Radnor, who added two detached wings between 1693 and 1705. In 1710 Wimpole was sold again to the Duke of Newcastle, but passed rapidly to his son-in-law Edward Harley, 2nd Earl of Oxford, who, between 1713 and 1721, engaged James Gibbs to remodel the house.

Gibbs added two wings. The one to the east is a chapel, and in 1724 this was painted in the grand Baroque manner by Sir James Thornhill, the main scene being a large *Adoration of the Magi* on the altar wall. Thornhill was the only native-born artist of the day who could compete with the many foreign decorative painters who worked in England at this time. His greatest triumph was beating his rivals in the competition for the commission to paint the dome of St Paul's Cathedral.

The library was built by Gibbs to house Edward Harley's immense library, known as the Harleian Collection. It was sold after his death, the manuscripts going to the British Museum.

In 1740 Wimpole was bought by Philip Yorke, 1st Earl of Hardwicke, Lord Chancellor and leading statesman of his day. He commissioned Henry Flitcroft to reface the house, create a long gallery and rebuild the nearby parish church. The 3rd Earl was a friend of the architect Sir John

The grandeur of Wimpole Hall is emphasized by its position on a low hill

Soane, and in the 1790s Soane designed the Book Room as an ante-room to the library and the dramatic 'T'-shaped Yellow Drawing Room, which soars through the full height of the house and is lit by a glass dome. Soane went on to design a bath-house, which displays his masterly handling of complex, yet simply ornamented, round-arched spaces. Baths of this sort were used principally for health reasons (as at spa towns) rather than for cleanliness.

By the early 20th century the house had fallen into a derelict condition and – apart from the Yellow Drawing Room suite and some marble-topped side-tables – was virtually empty until it was bought by Captain George Bambridge in 1938. In her widowhood, his wife, the daughter of Rudyard Kipling, set about collecting furniture and *objets d'art* with which to restore the house. The paintings include works by Reynolds, Ramsay, Cotes, Bonington and Tissot, and the bedrooms have pretty 19th-century wallpapers and a comfortable array of period furnishings.

8 miles (13 km) south-west of
Cambridge, off the A603 (map page 55)

WOBURN ABBEY   BEDFORDSHIRE

Large as it is, Woburn Abbey, home of the Duke of Bedford, was, until 1950, almost twice its present size (the east wing was riddled with dry rot and demolished). It has been the home of the Russell family since 1547, when the site was acquired from the old Cistercian Abbey by Lord John Russell, the 1st Earl of Bedford. The Earl concentrated his interests on Chenies Manor in Buckinghamshire, and Woburn did not figure highly in family affairs until the 4th Earl, Francis, moved there in 1619.

The house was largely rebuilt by Henry Flitcroft between 1747 and 1761. He added the west side of the house, with its broad, central portico, and refashioned the Jacobean north wing. However, Flitcroft was not the most exciting of architects and Woburn impresses by scale rather than beauty. Henry Holland was employed by the 5th Duke at the end of the century, and it was his fourth side of the square that was demolished in 1950 because of rampant dry rot. Tragic though this loss was, such is the enormity of the building that its latterday reduction is unnoticed.

Woburn has many treasures and a picture collection which is justly famous. As with most large country houses, there are many English portraits, but Woburn has something special in George Gower's picture of Elizabeth I shown triumphant over the Spanish Armada. The most remarkable feature of the picture collection, however, is a room containing 24 Canalettos. Notable pieces of French furniture by Montigny, Riesener and Langlois stand in Flitcroft's state rooms. The Chinese Room has beautiful hand-painted Chinese wallpaper and some fine Chinese Chippendale furniture. This chinoiserie theme is continued in the grounds in the Chinese Dairy, an exquisite oriental folly of pagoda roofs and elegant fretwork which overlooks a beautiful pond of lilies.

Woburn was opened to the public in 1955 and since then has become acknowledged as the supreme example of a stately home commercialized as a mass attraction. Its allurements include wildlife (as with LONGLEAT, Wiltshire) and its popularity can be seen by the enormous number of visitors it has annually.

5 miles (8 km) north of Leighton
Buzzard, at the junction of the A418,
A5130 and B528 (map page 55)

Opening Times

—◆—

Note Current opening times are given, but these may be subject to change. Before making a special journey to visit a particular country house, it may be best to check that it will be open.

ABBOTSFORD
Mid March to end October: Monday to Saturday 10–5; Sunday 2–5

ALTHORP
September to June: daily 1–5. July to August: daily 11–6. Bank holidays 11–6

ANGLESEY ABBEY
Easter to mid October: Wednesday to Sunday and bank holiday Monday 1.30–5.30. Closed Good Friday

ANTONY HOUSE
April to end October: Tuesday, Wednesday, Thursday and bank holiday Monday, plus Sunday in June, July and August 2–6. Last guided tour 5.30 pm

ARBURY HALL
Sunday from Easter Sunday to end September; bank holiday Monday, Tuesday and Wednesday in July and August: 2–5.30

ATHELHAMPTON
Easter to end October: 2–6 on Wednesday, Thursday and Sunday, Good Friday and bank holidays; also Monday and Tuesday in August 2–6

ATTINGHAM PARK
Easter to end September: Saturday to Wednesday 1.30–5; Sunday and bank holiday Monday 11–5. Closed Good Friday. October: Saturday and Sunday 1.30–5

BARRINGTON COURT
Mid April to mid October: Wednesday only 2–5

BELTON HOUSE
Easter to end October: Wednesday to Sunday and bank holiday Monday (closed Good Friday) 1–5.30

BELVOIR CASTLE
Mid March to mid October: Tuesday, Wednesday, Thursday, Friday, Saturday, Sunday 11–7; bank holiday Monday 11–7. October: Saturday and Sunday only 11–6

BERRINGTON HALL
April: Saturday, Sunday and Easter Monday 1.30–5.30. May to end September: Wednesday to Sunday and bank holiday Monday 1.30–5.30. October: Saturday and Sunday 1.30–4.30

BLENHEIM PALACE
Mid March to end October; daily 10.30–5.30

BLICKLING HALL
Easter to end October: Tuesday, Wednesday, Friday, Saturday, Sunday and bank holiday Monday 1–5. Closed Good Friday

BOUGHTON HOUSE
End July to end August: daily 12–6

BROADLANDS
Mid April to end September: daily 10–5.30. Closed Friday (except Good Friday) until 1 August

BROUGHTON CASTLE
Mid May to mid September: Wednesday and Sunday 2–5; also Thursday in July and August 2–5. Bank holiday Sunday and bank holiday Monday including Easter 2–5

BRYMPTON D'EVERCY
Easter weekend (Friday to Monday inclusive), then May to end September: daily (except Thursday and Friday) 2–6

BURGHLEY HOUSE
Daily from Good Friday to mid October 11–5; Good Friday 2–5

BURTON CONSTABLE
Easter Sunday and Monday; spring bank holiday Sunday and Monday; May Day Sunday and Monday; Sunday in June and July; mid July to early September (Sunday to Thursday) inclusive: 1–4.30

CALKE ABBEY
Easter to end October: Saturday to Wednesday including bank holiday Monday 12.30–5 (closed Good Friday)

CASTELL COCH
Easter to mid October: daily 9.30–6.30. From mid October to Easter: weekdays 9.30–4; Sunday 2–4

CASTLE HOWARD
Mid March to early November: daily. House and Costume Galleries open from 11 am

CHARLECOTE PARK
April to end October: daily (except Monday and Thursday) 11–6 (open bank holiday Monday 11–6). Closed Good Friday

CHATSWORTH
Mid March to end October: daily 11–4.30

CHICHELEY HALL
Mid April to end May, and early August to early September: Monday 2.30–6. Last tour 5 pm

CHISWICK HOUSE
Good Friday or 1 April (whichever is earlier) to 30 September: daily 10–6. 1 October to Maundy Thursday or 31 March (whichever is earlier): daily 10–4 (including Boxing Day and New Year's Day)

CLAYDON HOUSE
Easter to end October: Saturday to Wednesday 1–5; bank holiday Monday 1–5. Closed Good Friday

CORSHAM COURT
State rooms 1 January to 30 November: daily except Monday and Friday 2–4.30. From Good Friday to 30 September 2–6 (including Friday and bank holidays). Closed December

COTEHELE HOUSE
Easter to end October: daily (except Friday) 11–6; 11–5 in October. Open Good Friday

CRAGSIDE
Easter to end October: daily (except Monday) 1–5.30. Last admission 5 pm. Open bank holiday Monday

CULZEAN CASTLE
April to end October: daily 10.30–5

DORNEY COURT
Easter weekend Friday to Monday, then Sunday and bank holiday Monday to end May; also Sunday, Monday and Tuesday in June, July, August and September 2–5

DRUMLANRIG CASTLE
End April to early September: weekdays 11–5 (closed Thursday) and Sunday 1–5

DYRHAM PARK
Easter to early November: daily (except Thursday and Friday) 12–5.30

ELTON HALL
Easter Sunday and Monday 2–5. Bank holidays during May and August: Sunday and Monday 2–5. July: Wednesday and Sunday 2–5. August: Wednesday, Thursday and Sunday 2–5

ERDDIG
Good Friday to mid October: daily except Thursday and Friday 12–5. Open bank holiday Monday

FELBRIGG HALL
Easter to end October: Monday, Wednesday, Thursday, Saturday and Sunday 1.30–5.30

FORDE ABBEY
Good Friday to end October: Wednesday, Sunday and bank holidays 1–4.30

HADDON HALL
Easter to end September: daily (except Monday) 11–6. Closed Sunday in July and August

HAGLEY HALL
Daily during Easter weekend, spring bank holiday and August bank holiday weekends 2–5

HAM HOUSE
House closed for major repairs from August 1991 to the spring of 1993, during which time the garden will remain open as normal (daily except Monday, Christmas Day, Boxing Day and New Year's Day 11–5.30)

HARDWICK HALL
Easter to end October: Wednesday, Thursday, Saturday, Sunday and bank holiday Monday 12.30–5 or sunset if earlier (closed Good Friday)

HAREWOOD HOUSE
Mid March to end October: open daily at 11 am; closing times vary, but from mid May to early September closes at 5.45 pm

HATFIELD HOUSE
Mid March to mid October: Tuesday to Saturday (guided tours only) 12–4.15; Sunday (no guided tours) 1.30–5; bank holiday Monday (no guided tours) 11–5

HEVER CASTLE
Mid March to mid November: daily 12–6. Last admission 5.15 pm

HOLKHAM HALL
End May to end September: daily (except Friday and Saturday) 1.30–5; also Easter, May, spring and summer bank holidays: Sunday and Monday 11.30–5

HOPETOUN HOUSE
Easter weekend: daily 10–5.30. End April to end September: daily 10–5.30

HOUGHTON HALL
Easter Sunday to end September: Sunday, Thursday and bank holidays 1–5.30. Last admission 5 pm

ICKWORTH
Easter to end April and October: weekends only and bank holiday Monday 1.30–5.30. May to September: Tuesday, Wednesday,

Friday, Saturday, Sunday and bank holiday Monday 1.30–5.30

IGHTHAM MOTE
Easter to end October: daily (except Tuesday and Saturday): weekdays 12–5.30; Sunday and bank holidays 11–5.30. Last admission 5 pm

INVERARAY CASTLE
First Saturday in April to second Sunday in October. April, May, June, September and October: 10–1 and 2–6 (Castle stays open 1–2 in June); Sunday 1–6; closed Friday. July and August: daily 10–6 (including Friday); Sunday 1–6

KEDLESTON HALL
Easter to end October: Saturday to Wednesday 1–5.30

KENWOOD HOUSE
Good Friday or April (whichever is earlier) to 30 September: daily 10–6. 1 October to Maundy Thursday or 31 March: daily 10–4 (including Boxing Day and New Year's Day)

KINGSTON LACY
Mid March to early November: daily (except Thursday and Friday) 12–5.30

KINGSTON LISLE
Not generally open to the public, although special visits may be arranged by permission of the owner

KNOLE
Easter to end October: Wednesday to Saturday, bank holiday Monday and Good Friday 11–5; Sunday 2–5

LACOCK ABBEY
Easter to early November: daily (except Tuesday) 1–5.30

LANHYDROCK
Easter to end October: daily (except Monday) 11–6; bank holiday

Monday 11–6. Closes 5 pm in October

LEVENS HALL
Easter Sunday to 30 September: Sunday to Thursday 11–5

LITTLE MORETON HALL
March and October: Saturday and Sunday 1.30–5.30; April to end September: daily (except Tuesday) 1.30–5.30; bank holiday Monday 11.30–5.30

LONGLEAT
Easter to 30 September 10–6; rest of year 10–4. Closed Christmas Day

LOSELEY HOUSE
End May to end September: Wednesday, Thursday, Friday and Saturday 2–5; also summer bank holiday Monday 2–5

LYME PARK
Good Friday to end September. Mid May to early June, and mid July to end August: daily except Monday and Friday (but open bank holiday Monday) 2–5. Guided tours only: end March to mid May, mid June to mid July, and September: Tuesday, Wednesday, Thursday 2–4 hourly, Saturday half-hourly, Sunday free-flow 2–5. Last admission 4.15 pm

LYTES CARY
April (or Easter if earlier) to end October: Monday, Wednesday and Saturday 2–6 (or dusk if earlier)

MELLERSTAIN
Good Friday to Easter Monday, then 1 May to end September: daily (except Saturday) 12.30–5

MILTON MANOR
Easter Saturday to end September: Saturday and Sunday 2–5.30

MOCCAS COURT
April to end September: Thursday only 2–6

MONTACUTE HOUSE
Easter to early November: daily (except Tuesday) 12–5.30

NEWBY HALL
Easter to end September: Tuesday to Sunday and bank holiday Monday 12–5

NEWSTEAD ABBEY
Good Friday to September: daily 12–6

NOSTELL PRIORY
Easter to end October as follows – April, May, June, September and October: Saturday 12–5; Sunday 11–5. July and August: daily (except Friday) 12–5; Sunday 11–5. Bank holidays as follows – Easter Monday and Tuesday (closed Good Friday), May Day Monday, spring bank holiday Monday and Tuesday, August bank holiday Monday: 11–5 on Monday; 12–5 on Tuesday

OSTERLEY PARK
Easter to end October: Wednesday to Friday 1–5; Saturday, Sunday and bank holiday Monday 11–5. Closed Good Friday

PENCARROW
Easter to mid October: daily except Friday and Saturday 1.30–5 (June to mid September and bank holiday Monday 11–5)

PENSHURST PLACE
Easter to end September: daily (except Monday) 1–5.30. Open all bank holidays in season

PETWORTH
Easter to end October: daily (except Monday and Friday) 1–5.30. Tuesday, Wednesday and Thursday:

extra rooms shown. Open Good Friday and bank holiday Monday (closed Tuesday following)

SCALE POLESDEN LACEY
March and November: Saturday and Sunday only 1.30–4.30. Easter to end October: Wednesday to Sunday (including Good Friday) 1.30–5.30. Also open bank holiday Monday and preceding Sunday 11–5.30

RAGLEY HALL
Easter to end September: daily except Monday and Friday (but open bank holiday Monday) 12–5

ROUSHAM PARK
April to end September: Wednesday, Sunday and bank holidays 2–4.30

ST MICHAEL'S MOUNT
Easter to end October: Monday to Friday 10.30–5.45. November to end March: guided tours as tide, weather and circumstances permit 10.30–5.45

SALTRAM
Easter to end October: daily except Friday and Saturday (open bank holiday Friday and Saturday) 12.30–6, but closes at 5 pm in October

SEZINCOTE
May, June, July and September: Thursday and Friday only 2.30–6

SHERBORNE CASTLE
Easter Saturday to end September: Thursday, Saturday, Sunday and bank holiday Monday 2–6

SHUGBOROUGH
Good Friday to end October: daily 11–5. Then November to just before Christmas, and 2 January to Easter: weekdays 10.30–4

SLEDMERE HOUSE
Early May to end September: daily

(except Monday and Friday) 1.30–5; also Easter and Sunday in April, and bank holiday Monday

SQUERRYES COURT
March: Sunday only 2–6. April to September: Wednesday, Saturday, Sunday and bank holiday Monday 2–6

STANWAY MANOR
June, July and August: Tuesday and Thursday 2–5

STOKESAY CASTLE
From first Wednesday in March: daily (except Tuesday) 10–5. April to September: daily (except Tuesday) 10–6. October: daily (except Tuesday) 10–5. November: weekends only 10–3

STONOR PARK
April: Sunday and bank holiday Monday only; May, June and September: Wednesday, Sunday and bank holiday Monday; July: Wednesday, Thursday and Sunday; August: Wednesday, Thursday, Saturday, Sunday and bank holiday Monday 2–5.30 (bank holiday Monday 11–5.30)

STOURHEAD
Mid March to early November: daily (except Thursday and Friday) 12–5.30 (or dusk if earlier)

STRATFIELD SAYE
May to last Sunday in September: daily (except Friday) 11.30–4

SUDBURY HALL
Easter to end October: Wednesday to Sunday and bank holiday Monday 12.30–5 (or sunset if earlier). Closed Good Friday

SYON HOUSE
Easter to end October: Sunday to

Thursday 12–5 (Sunday only in October)

THE VYNE
Easter to end October: Tuesday, Wednesday, Thursday, Saturday and Sunday 1.30–5.30. Open Good Friday and bank holiday Monday 11.30–5.30 (closed Tuesday following)

WADDESDON MANOR
House closed for refurbishment during 1991 and 1992, opening again in 1993. Grounds and aviary remain open

WALLINGTON
Easter to end October: daily (except Tuesday) 1–5.30

WESTON PARK
Easter to early June: weekends only. Bank holidays, Easter week, spring bank holiday week, early June to end July: daily (except Monday and Friday); end July to end August: daily, then weekends only until end September. Park 11–7

WEST WYCOMBE PARK
June, July and August: Sunday to Thursday, and bank holidays 2–5

WILTON HOUSE
Easter to mid October: Tuesday to Saturday and bank holiday Monday 11–6; Sunday 1–6

WIMPOLE HALL
Easter to early November: Tuesday, Wednesday, Thursday, Saturday and Sunday 1–5 (open bank holiday Sunday and Monday 11–5)

WOBURN ABBEY
January to mid March: weekends only 11–4. Then mid March to early November: weekdays 11–5; Sunday and bank holidays 11–5.30

Glossary of Architectural Terms

arabesque an ornamental motif featuring scrolling or interlacing plant forms

architrave in classical architecture, the horizontal feature that rests directly on top of a row of columns, forming the lowest part of the entablature; the term 'architrave' can also refer to a decorative moulding around a door or window

Arts and Crafts movement a late 19th-century artistic movement that emphasized craftsmanship in the face of growing mass-production

attic in classical architecture, a low subsidiary storey above the main entablature of a building; in everyday usage the term also refers to a room directly under the roof of a house

Baronial/Scottish Baronial style a style of architecture popular for Scottish country houses in the 19th century, based on a romantic evocation of the country's martial past, with much display of turrets and battlements

Baroque a style of architecture (and other arts) prevalent in the 17th and early 18th centuries. It is a style of extravagant display and in a full-blooded form was popular only briefly in Britain – this was partly because it had associations with Catholicism that were unacceptable in Protestant countries

barrel vault a vault shaped like the roof of a tunnel (it is indeed sometimes called a tunnel vault)

belvedere a building (or part of a building) situated to command a fine view

Chinese Chippendale a type of chinoiserie furniture associated with Thomas Chippendale, who illustrated it in his book *The Gentleman & Cabinet-Maker's Director*

(1754); it is rather angular in outline, often with lattice-work ornament – much less elaborate and fanciful than much chinoiserie

chinoiserie the evocation or imitation of Chinese styles in European art and architecture; the term is applied mainly to the whimsical and often highly-ornate type of pseudo-Chinese decoration popular in furniture and interior design in the 18th century

classical architecture a very general term covering all styles of architecture that use the forms and decorative treatments established in ancient Greece and Rome, particularly the orders; it is subdivided into more specific styles, such as Baroque and neo-classicism

cornice a decorative horizontal projection running along a wall or other surface; also the top part of an entablature

crenellation another term for battlements

cupola a dome, particularly a small decorative dome surmounting a roof

curtain wall a wall connecting two towers or similar structures

dormer a window projecting from the slope of a roof

enfilade a system of aligning a series of doors connecting a suite of rooms so that when they are all open a vista is obtained through them

entablature in classical architecture, a group of three horizontal decorative bands (architrave, frieze and cornice) surmounting a column or group of columns

eyecatcher a building designed purely to provide a striking feature in a view, often built on an elevated point in a landscape garden; it is a type of 'folly' and the two terms are often used more or less synonymously

folly a building or structure built purely for decoration, often as a garden ornament

gable a triangular or roughly triangular section of outer wall forming or embellishing the end of a sloping roof. The sides were often decoratively curved, particularly in 17th-century houses. (A 'bell gable' is so called because it resembles a bell in outline; a 'Dutch gable' is topped by an arch or pediment. The two types are not always clearly distinguished)

gazebo a summerhouse or garden pavilion, particularly one looking out over a pleasant view

girandole a candelabrum, especially one attached to a wall and backed with a mirror (*see also sconce*)

Gothic the style of architecture predominant in the late Middle Ages; its most obvious characteristic is the use of pointed arches

Gothick a term sometimes applied to the type of pseudo-Gothic architecture and decoration popular in the 18th century; it was picturesque and lighthearted, with none of the serious archaeological spirit that characterized Gothic Revival architecture in the 19th century

Gothic Revival a movement in architecture and associated arts in which the medieval Gothic style was revived. It began in the 18th century in a carefree rococo spirit and culminated in the 19th century

Grand Tour a lengthy journey to the Continent (in particular Italy) that was considered an almost obligatory part of the education of the British gentleman in the 18th century. Many country houses contain treasures collected on the Grand Tour

grisaille a painting in shades of grey or another neutral colour, such as dull green; grisaille paintings often imitate the effect of sculptural decoration

grotesque a type of wall decoration using fanciful interlinked human, animal and plant motifs. The name derives from Roman buildings called *grotte* in which such decoration was discovered during the Renaissance. It was a popular form of ornament in painting, carving and stucco in the 16th, 17th and 18th centuries

hipped roof a roof in which the ends slope inwards rather than rising vertically

Lady Chapel a chapel dedicated to the Virgin Mary

lancet a tall, narrow, pointed-headed window – a typical feature of early Gothic architecture

linenfold a type of carved panelling featuring a repeated pattern resembling a loosely folded linen napkin. It was extremely popular in interior decoration in the Tudor period

loggia a gallery open to the air on one or more sides

louvre a slatted opening for ventilation

marquetry decorative inlay in wood, ivory or other suitable materials, principally on furniture

minstrel gallery in medieval and Tudor houses, a projecting platform or balcony overlooking the hall

moulding a projecting or recessed band of ornament on a wall or other surface. The various different styles of architecture have typical mouldings, some simple, others highly elaborate

mullion a vertical strip of stone or other material dividing a window into separate panes or 'lights'

neo-classicism the predominant movement in European art in the late 18th and early 19th centuries, marked by a desire to revive the forms and spirit of the art of ancient Greece and Rome. Other styles had already looked to antique art for inspiration, but neo-classicism went beyond them in seeking archaeological exactness of detail and a lofty tone considered worthy of the most venerable sources

neo-Gothic an alternative name for Gothic Revival

ogee an arch with an 'S'-shaped curve on both sides, joining at the top in a point

order in classical architecture, a unit or system of design based on the type of column used. Each order consists of the column plus the entablature it supports and its pedestal (if any). The ancient Greeks used three orders – Doric, Ionic and Corinthian – which became progressively slimmer and more decorative. To these the Romans added Tuscan (a simpler form of Doric) and Composite (the most lavish of all, combining some of the features of Ionic and Corinthian). The orders were regarded as the heart of classical architecture and their proportioning and detailing were studied and codified with great care in numerous books. There was a kind of architectural etiquette in their use, so that, for example, when two or more orders were used together, the 'lighter', more decorative ones were placed above the 'heavier', more sober ones

oriel a bay window projecting from an upper storey

ormolu gilded bronze used for ornamental objects, to decorate furniture etc

Palladianism a movement in architecture and interior design based on the buildings and writings of the great Italian architect Andrea Palladio (1508–80). The term can be applied to any avowed imitation of Palladio's work, but most often it is used of British architecture in the period *c.*1715–*c.*1750 when Palladianism was the dominant style. It was marked by regularity, symmetry and purity of detailing; exteriors were generally fairly severe, but interiors were often very rich

Perpendicular the final phase of Gothic architecture in England, originating in about 1330 and continuing into the 16th century, when it began to mingle with Renaissance influence. Perpendicular is so called because of the vertical emphasis in window tracery and other elements of design. It was mainly a style of church architecture, but features of it are commonly found in domestic buildings

piano nobile an Italian term for the main floor of a building, containing the reception rooms. In Britain it is mainly applied to Palladian mansions

Picturesque an aesthetic movement in the late 18th and early 19th centuries relating to natural landscape, garden design, architecture and painting. Advocates of the Picturesque took delight in roughness and irregularity

pier glass a tall mirror occupying the wall space between two windows; pier glasses were particularly popular in the 18th century

pilaster a flat pillar projecting only slightly from a wall; pilasters are usually decorative rather than structural

Pre-Raphaelite Brotherhood a group of young English artists who banded together in 1848 with the aim of recapturing the sincerity and simplicity of Italian art before the time of Raphael (1483–1520)

quatrefoil a decorative motif with four lobes (rather like a four-leaved clover)

Queen Anne style the style of unpretentious red-brick architecture seen in many English houses of the late 17th and early 18th centuries. It began some time before the reign of Queen Anne (1702–14), after whom it is named

Renaissance a term referring to the rebirth of classical taste that began in Italy in the 15th century. In architecture it refers specifically to a return to the decorative features of Roman architecture in place of the medieval Gothic style. In Britain the Gothic and Renaissance styles mingled in the 16th century

rococo a style of art and architecture that succeeded the Baroque style in the 18th century. It was characterized by lightness, grace and playfulness

rustication stonework with a roughly textured surface or cut with deep channels between the blocks. It is used on lower storeys to give a feeling of rugged strength

sash/sliding sash window a window with two movable frames (sashes) that can be made to slide up or down by means of pulleys

sconce a decorative wall bracket for holding candles. The terms 'sconce' and 'girandole' are not always clearly distinguished

screens passage in a medieval or Tudor house, the space between the screen in the hall and the entrances to the kitchen, buttery and pantry

solar in a medieval or Tudor house, a private room for the owner's family, away from the hubbub of the hall

strapwork ornament resembling leather or parchment strips that have been elaborately cut and pierced

stucco a type of plaster mixed with powdered marble and glue, used for sculpture and architectural decoration

torchère a tall stand for supporting candlesticks

tracery decorative stonework in window openings, a characteristic feature of Gothic architecture. The term is also applied to similar decoration on furniture

trompe-l'œil a painting (or part of one) intended to deceive the spectator into thinking it is a real object rather than a two-dimensional representation of it (the term is French for 'deceives the eye')

Index

Acknowledgements

———◆———

The author wishes to thank Peter Sinclair of the Historic Houses Association for his assistance and advice.

The photographs in *Country Houses* were supplied by the photographers and agencies listed below:
AA Photolibrary pp. 77, 87, 133, 138
Jeffrey Beazley pp. 27, 81, 88, 117, 142
John Bethell pp. 2, 6, 11, 17, 19, 20, 22, 25, 30, 32, 34, 37, 38, 42, 44, 47, 52, 58 (and front cover), 60, 64, 68, 79, 82, 84, 93, 100, 102, 124, 126, 128, 136
Impact Photos/Tony Page p. 145; Pamla Toler p. 97
Marianne Majerus pp. 15, 72
National Trust Photographic Library/John Blake p. 122; Nick Carter p. 110; Nick Daly p. 98; Mark Fiennes p. 105; Rob Matheson p. 8; Mike Williams p. 75
Robert O'Dea p. 49
The line drawings are by Lyn Cawley, and the house illustrations in the gazetteer are by Sheilagh Noble.
The maps on pp. 54–7 were drawn by John Gilkes.